MW00386638

PRAISE FOR *GROWING DESPERATE*

"One of the biggest dangers for the Western Christian is to wrap our lives in so much bubble wrap, that we no longer remain vulnerable, raw, broken and, most of all, dependent upon Jesus. Mike carefully removes the bubble wrap we have put around our own souls as he reminds us that it's only in our desperation that we can fully meet the perfect love that saves us. *Growing Desperate* reminds us that, in the same way Jesus noticed the desperate hemorrhaging woman, He notices our own, everyday brokenness as well, if only we would be desperate enough to reach up. After reading this book, you will be."

> — **Jessica Honegger**, founder and CEO of Noonday Collection and author of *Imperfect Courage*

"*Growing Desperate* offers a most inspiring and compelling insight into Jesus' promise of the kingdom for the poor in spirit. It's well-written and chock-full of fascinating stories of Mike's experiences from his life and the lives of people he's served both in the U.S. and Indonesia. His winsome, transparent style of writing invites the reader to be more than okay with our own neediness. Most refreshing is Mike's call for us not to just look inward but to also look outward to others who are needy. Mike lives what he's addressing in his book, thus it carries much authority."

> — **Ron Parrish**, author of *Building Your Spiritual Core* and *From Duty to Delight*

"Mike O'Quin is equal parts storyteller and theologian. His writing is crisp and relatable, his stories are engaging, and he unpacks the Scripture with the insight of a seasoned pastor. *Growing Desperate* poses one of the most troubling central questions of my faith journey, 'Where is God when I feel desperate and alone?' It's a question we've all asked, and Mike provides an answer we all need to read for ourselves."

> — **Rob Stennett**, author of *The Almost True Story of Ryan Fisher* and *The Perfect Dad*

"There are generally two types of writers who fill the pages of books in stores. The first are famous people who need some help to make their story readable. You'll buy the book 'cause you know who they are but struggle to finish reading their passable drivel. The second are people you've never heard of who have ridiculous writing talent. Imagery leaps off the page so vivid and real you forget you're reading. You're living the story. You can't wait to read more, wished it wouldn't end and ache to read it again. Mike O'Quin is that second type of writer. Even better, he's lived desperation from Austin to Indonesia. You'll feel his stories tugging at your soul. More importantly, you'll hear the voice of God calling you to a life that's richer, riskier and singing a new song."

> — **Peter Nevland**, author of *Exposing the Psalms* and *I'm Going to be a Zebra*

"A much needed message for all who have come to the end of themselves and have realized their brokenness and desperation. Mike O'Quin eloquently shares how those who have exhausted themselves spiritually, emotionally, and relationally can find rest and healing for their weary souls. *Growing Desperate* is an excellent, moving explanation of both the heart of God and the Gospel. A highly recommended read that is sure to bless believers at every stage of life."

— **R. Duncan Williams**, author of the *Thinkwave series*

"Mike is a great communicator whether he is speaking, writing, or just in a group at lunch telling stories. Mike is also vulnerable and honest. He is good at opening up his own life and struggling with how he is doing at pursing his deepest values more than 20 years into his walk with Jesus in pastoral ministry and as a missionary. *Growing Desperate* will bring a challenge and comfort to you as the reader, or to a friend who really needs the encouragement."

— **Mark Buckner**, pastor, Community of Faith Christian Fellowship, Boston

"Honesty is what you will find as you advance through the treasures that await you in this unforgettable book. The words are not the hollow ramblings of an academic, but rather the wisdom of a man who writes from the depths of his quest to find meaning and hope in the darkest and loneliest circumstances you have ever endured. My life has been profoundly and deeply shaken by my friendship with Mike O'Quin. I invite you to read his meditations on human desperation. Prepare your heart. I dare say, you will never be the same."

— **Paul Richardson**, *author of A Certain Risk: Living Your Faith at the Edge*

Growing Desperate

The Favor of God for the Poor in Spirit

Mike O'Quin Jr.

MANTAP
PUBLISHING

Copyright © 2016 Mike O'Quin Jr.

All Scripture quotations, unless otherwise indicated, are taken from the Holy Bible, *New International Version* ®, NIV ® Copyright © 1973, 1978, 1984, 2011 by Biblica, Inc.® Used by permission. All rights reserved worldwide.

Scriptures Scripture quotations marked NASB are taken from the *New American Standard Bible* ®, Copyright © 1960, 1962, 1963, 1968, 1971, 1972, 1973, 1975, 1977, 1995 by The Lockman Foundation. Used by permission.

Cover design by Joshua Kazemi • joshuakazemi.com

Cover photo by Caio Freitas • cviophotos.com

Contact the author on his blog: mikeoquin.com

Mantap Publishing • mantappublishing.com

All rights reserved

Library of Congress Control Number: 2016912362
ISBN: 0692761187
ISBN-13: 978-0692761182

For Stephanie

Kind, Beautiful, Gracious, Courageous

CONTENTS

Prologue

Part I • Toward Him

One • Dichotomy and Desperation

Two • The Spiritually Desperate

Three • The Emotionally Desperate

Four • The Relationally Desperate

Five • Desperate for Community

Part II • For Them

Six • Intentional Desperation

Seven • The Poor

Eight • The Grieving

Nine • The Lost

Epilogue • Rescue

PROLOGUE

———————

The doctor poked his head out of the body bag, his only solace from the slicing rain, and tugged on my bag with his jittery hand. My head emerged out of my own plastic cocoon as I squinted with reddened eyes in his direction.

"Do you see everyone's lips?" he shouted over the rain pounding the deck of the small shrimp boat. "Do you see them trembling?"

I looked over at my quivering teammates in their body bags, closed off at the top by their own white-knuckled hands, all of them packed in tight sardine-like rows on the drenched deck. Stacks of bags were on board in case we needed to retrieve corpses, but so far we hadn't seen any. In light of the circumstances, we figured it was okay to borrow the plastic shelters temporarily. Every now and then a top would open, a head would pop out and vomit would shoot from a delirious mouth. We had all stopped going to the side of the boat hours ago to relieve our seasickness. The boat creaked and moaned as the roaring waves of the Indian Ocean splashed overboard and mocked us.

The only face I could make out was that of a nurse protecting herself from the rain in the plastic bag next to me. Indeed, her lips were trembling and I nodded my affirmation to the good doctor's question.

"We are getting hypothermia," his hoarse voice announced. "When we get to the village we are not going to be any good for anyone."

I processed this most recent item of bad news before he requested, "Can you ask the crew how much longer? I don't think we can take much more of this."

Reluctantly, I opened my flimsy shelter and braved the chilling rain to get some answers. A crewman was navigating his way across the deck of the boat toward the stern. "*Mas*," I asked him in Indonesian, "How much longer?"

He looked toward the darkened horizon, as if he could summon the answer directly from the storm, and plainly informed me, "eight more hours."

Well that couldn't be right. It had already been eight hours and it was supposed to be only eight hours total to our village. I would need to talk to the man in charge, the captain. Making my way to an oil drum that served as the vessel's only ladder, I hoisted my sopping body atop it as my weight tilted it and gasoline sloshed out onto the deck. I struggled along the narrow edge, hoping I wouldn't fall and land on top of someone, or worse, overboard into the churning ocean. I finally made it to the captain's bridge, if that's what you could call the closet-sized room. Space was tight on this 18-foot vessel, built for five experienced crewmen, not a team of 24 Indonesian and American church volunteers turned relief workers.

I squeezed myself into the room packed with smoking crewmen and the captain gazing behind the wheel into the sightless horizon. I delivered the message from the doctor, in Indonesian, that we couldn't take much more of this. I reminded him that it had already been eight hours, the estimated time for the entire journey, and that most of our team was getting sick.

"I don't think we can make it to Tuenom," I concluded to the captain, who didn't seem very sympathetic to my complaints and kept his eye on the choppy sea. "Is there a way we can just dock in some other village along the coast?"

"No. The tsunami destroyed those villages," he explained without emotion, still without looking in my direction. "There is too much debris in the sea and I couldn't do it anyway in this storm."

I warmed myself with a tight self-hug and cautioned into the next question. "How about if we just headed back to Banda Aceh for the night?"

He took his eyes off the sea and shot me a cold, caustic stare. "That's eight hours back." The other crewmen shared their consternation to my ignorant suggestion with muffled snorts.

Last question, and I really didn't want to know the answer. "Okay, then, how much longer do you estimate before we get to Tuenom."

"Eight more hours." The official confirmation pummeled my gut more than the pounding rain and seasickness combined.

Getting to this point in our journey from Central Texas to Aceh, Indonesia, had already taken a lot out of our team. Asking them to hang in there for eight more hours, sleep-deprived and wet and cold and seasick and huddled in body bags, was more than I could even suggest for a group of miserable people starting to get hypothermia. We had been promised at the start of this journey that we would be in Teunom way before nightfall. No one imagined a relentless storm of this caliber that seemed hell-bent on blocking us from our destination. It's hard to get hypothermia on the equator, but this storm seemed mighty enough to sicken and stop us.

He repeated his answer, *"delapan jam lagi,"* eight more hours, as if he could read my conflicted mind.

So eight more hours to go, eight more hours if we go back, and nothing to do but get sicker, wetter and colder. A couple of my teammates entered the tiny, shack-like room. I delivered the news, almost humorous at this point with its unbelievable audacity. Surely this nightmare couldn't have another chapter.

As my wide-eyed teammates processed our new estimated arrival time, I prayed under my breath, "O God, you can make a way where there is no way."

I climbed back down from the oil drum onto the deck of the boat and suddenly felt nauseous. Leaning over the edge of the boat, I vomited out the rest of the rice and fish meal we had been served hours earlier when the day was still sunny and felt exciting and adventurous. Now I second guessed our decision to rent out this tiny boat to take our team to a village which we had heard had received no medical care. The cataclysmic tsunami of December 26, 2004, had obliterated the village of Teunom, killing half its 16,000 inhabitants. Here it was two weeks later. To get to this village, with impassible roads and bigger relief agencies getting the limited helicopter rides, this boat was simply the only way.

I stepped over the row of living corpses and made my way to the doctor who had sent me on this errand. Though I was not looking forward to delivering this depressing data, I knew as one of the team's translators I was responsible for giving the team unfiltered facts and letting them make their own decisions. I tugged on the plastic bag and got his attention.

"Eight more hours," I said as gently as I could.

"What?" he demanded, shooting his head all the way out of his bag. "There is no way we can take eight more hours of this." I totally agreed. But neither I nor any of the crew could offer any other options. The rain seemed to get even colder as I retreated inside my plastic shelter.

"Oh, Lord," I cried out again to the God of heaven from within my soggy body bag, "You can make a way where there is no way!"

Growing desperate.

No other options. You can't go back and it feels impossible to go forward. The gap between the freedom you long for and the hell you inhabit. How can you ever be rescued from this raging storm?

God did make a way where there was no way for our storm-tossed team on the Indian Ocean. I'll bookend this entire book with the resolution of that story.

But this book is for those still feeling seasick on their own rickety boats right now, being tossed around by the merciless waves of life. For those still breathing yet entombed inside a body bag of some addiction or dire strait or relational stalemate. You and I have a choice. *We can grow desperate or we can grow colder.* We can cry out to the Captain or we can stay in that body bag until it's too late and hypothermia sets into our souls.

It's also for those of us who have spent too much of our lives paddling in the calm waters, afraid to venture beyond the shallow harbors of safety. Those of us with too many options, the non-desperate. We who have gotten a little too comfy, with no real need to cry out to God for anything. Here's a test question...are you attempting anything for the kingdom of heaven right now that would utterly fail without the intervention of God?

Jesus said blessed (happy, downright favored by God) are the poor in spirit (Matthew 5:3). That word for poor—*ptōchos*—isn't blue collar, working class poor, but destitute, bombed out wretches clamoring for coins on the streets of Calcutta poor. These are the folks who just can't help themselves without a hand reaching down to them. Spiritual beggars are so favored by God because they have no other options. He loves lavishing on them the kingdom of heaven and making a way for them where there is no way. He loves being the God of hope for a people of desperation.

The good news is that Jesus is not waiting around for you to get your act together. He suffered and died for so much more than that. You can bring your broken life before Him, as is, and He delights to restore you so much that you actually become a life restorer.

Henry David Thoreau famously wrote that "the mass of men lead lives of quiet desperation and go to the grave with the song still in them."[1] My desire in the message of this book is that we would be inspired to lives of valiant desperation and go to the grave with the song in us fully sung.

Mike O'Quin Jr.
Austin, Texas

PART I

IN US

For this is what the high and lofty One says—
He who lives forever, whose name is holy:

> *"I live in a high and holy place,*
> *but also with him who is contrite and lowly in spirit,*
> *to revive the spirit of the lowly*
> *and to revive the heart of the contrite."*

— Isaiah 57:15

CHAPTER ONE

DICHOTOMY AND DESPERATION

"Can we talk about something?"

My wife, Stephanie, settled beside me on the couch and asked me this question. We had just finished cleaning up dinner dishes, guided our kids through their homework assignments and tucked them into bed for the night. I was looking forward to a little relaxation in front of the TV and definitely did not feel like talking about anything of substance.

I clicked the mute button on the remote and forced a half-smile. Her words started out sweetly and then she started fiddling with a piece of tissue in her hand and I knew I was in trouble. I was about to be CRITICIZED FOR SOMETHING. The alarm bells started going off. Batten down the hatches. Warning. Warning. Incoming critique.

She kindly let me know about some ways I had not been meeting her emotional needs as of late. She said she felt lonely in our relationship, like I was not really connecting with her on a heart level that much. "You're doing the right things and going through the motions," she explained, "But I just feel missed by you emotionally, like you're not really here. Your mind is always on something else. I feel this way a lot."

A defensive anger started rising in me. *Give me a break, lady. I'm just trying to relax here.* Then I started plotting my counter-attack. *Oh yeah? Why can't you be more appreciative of all I do? I do way more than most other husbands!*

We've had this conversation repeatedly, where she points out a disconnect between a value I profess (an emotionally attuned husband) and my day-to-day reality (distant, distracted hubby). She had the gall to call me out on an ideal that we both share for an emotionally intimate relationship.

In each of our lives we are frequently confronted by a dichotomy between the values we claim and the reality we have settled for. On that day I was guilty as charged for not living up to the biblical admonition for husbands to "be considerate as you live with your wives" (1 Peter 3:7).

Especially as believers, that dichotomy between the excellent ideals of the Scriptures and the slop of our reality can feel like the equidistance between heaven and earth. Thumb through your Bible for a few minutes and you will soon be confronted by a set of colossal standards. Serving selflessly. Living obediently. Giving generously. Walking in purity. Loving enemies. Seemingly impossible expectations like, hey, "Be perfect, therefore, as your heavenly Father is perfect" (Matthew 5:48).

If that weren't enough, we're also mandated to advance the kingdom of God on earth, to reach the lost, to lift the poor, to serve orphans and widows, and oh, don't forget world missions:

"Go into *all* the world and preach the good news to *all* creation" (Mark 16:15). Does that feel like a tall order to anybody?

With sky-high standards and daunting decrees like these, who isn't going to fall short? No wonder as believers we feel guilty so much of the time! Think over your own personal Good Christian List, depending on your particular denominational flavor. There is no way any of us are cutting it. Nowhere near.

What do we do with the gap between our professed values and our sub-par reality? As I see it, we have three options.

The Pushback of Defensiveness

The easiest choice is the one that I was tempted with on that sofa. Someone reminds me of how I am falling short on some category of my life and I want to immediately turn the tables on them. "I'm not meeting your needs? What about my needs? What about my need for encouragement? I'm not feeling very encouraged by you lately, especially now."

In other words, *the problem isn't me but you.* Your standards are just too high so give me a break here. Settle for a husband who is inconsiderate. Don't remind me of that dichotomy because I feel bad enough about myself already. Just be okay with the vegetated slouch on the sofa.

Do you get defensive easily? Maybe you've already made peace with your own sorry state of affairs and think others should, too. Take it easy on me because I'm only human, and you should know by now that humans aren't perfect. So back off. It's the attitude that would describe my strategy in my high school French class. My militant French teacher Mademoiselle Rich would pace in front of the class, daring volunteers to answer her latest Francophile grammar challenge. When no one would rise to take the bait, she would begin calling out names. Under her scorching gaze, I would hide my face behind the head in front of me, praying, "O God, don't let her call on me." Now that I think of it, it was probably the beginning of my prayer life.

Don't let anyone call on me. I'm keeping my head down because I want to be free to live with my own low standards and I want everyone else to be okay with that. Look away, Mademoiselle Rich, look away.

As I was writing this, Lionel Richie shuffled onto my playlist with his soothing song "Easy." He tried to soothe me into an easy Sunday morning life of settling: "I wanna be high, so high/I wanna be free to know the things I do are right." Earlier he says he's not happy when he tries to fake it, so geez people, lay off. This would be a great anthem for those of us who say don't call me on anything (because we're not happy when we try to fake it). Don't cramp my style by your insistence that I live up to my word. It would be a great song to sing to yourself as you are walking out of a commitment (but for the record, and even though it dates me, I still like that song).

This option does sound nice and easy, easy like a Sunday morning. But then we go back to the Bible and find themes of abundant life and overcoming: "No, in all these things we are more than conquerors through Him who loved us" (Romans 8:37). We know we are destined to thrive, not just survive: "...how much more will those who receive God's abundant provision of grace and of the gift of righteousness *reign in life* through the one man, Jesus Christ" (Romans 5:17).

We could choose this option, to settle for a life of settling, but a deep ache in our souls for abundant, thriving life would haunt our days.

The Cave-In of Self-Pity

Another option would be to agree with your adversary. *You're right, I should be living out Value X, but I'm really living Reality Y. Sigh.*

In this orientation, you feel bad that you're not living up to your own standards (*I should be a more caring husband*). Turning inwards, you condemn and beat yourself up. *They're right. I'm such a loser. What's wrong with me? Why can't I just…*

Personalities that orient toward the first option quickly turn on the defensive and demand that the dichotomy not be mentioned. *How rude of you to remind me of my failures!* But in this option you turn the fists inwards until your soul is bloodied and bruised. You at least go as far as admitting that the gap exists, but you stay mired in self-pity.

An inward orientation of condemnation is what the Bible calls "worldly sorrow." It may look humble, because there is sorrow over sin, but it's really a self-focused counterfeit:

> For you became sorrowful as God intended and so were not harmed in any way by us. Godly sorrow brings repentance that leads to salvation and leaves no regret, but worldly sorrow brings death. (2 Corinthians 7:9-10)

Worldly sorrow is sorry that it got caught, while godly sorrow looks to God for freedom and is eager to make things right. In this heartfelt letter, Paul continues to reach out to the people who he made sorry over their sin:

See what this godly sorrow has produced in you: what earnestness, what eagerness to clear yourselves, what indignation, what alarm, what longing, what concern, what readiness to see justice done...By all this we are encouraged. (2 Corinthians 7:11-13)

Paul was encouraged that the Corinthians got it. They weren't conned by the woe-is-me counterfeit sorrow that begins and ends in self. Anytime we are confronted with our shortcomings and stop at only feeling bad about them, it always leads to death. True repentance, believe it or not, requires a healthy dose of self-esteem.

We've got to get down to the roots of that sadness if our tendency is to hate ourselves over our deficiencies. In her honest book *Captivating,* Stasi Eldredge writes honestly about her own tendency to think that personal failures were "the truest thing" about her. God came through for her and spoke to her bruised heart:

He told me that the angels talk about me. I asked Him what they say. If you could hear them whisper in hushed and reverent voices, you would hear them say, "How beautiful, how glorious, how highly favored is she for whom the Son of God, the Lord of Glory chose to lay down His life."[2]

We know somewhere deep in our redeemed souls that we were destined for glory and not condemnation. As we tour through the New Testament, we sense that guilt is not the flavor. We're supposed to love ourselves, as in "love your neighbor as you love yourself" (Matthew 12:31), not despise ourselves. I dare say we're even supposed to *like* ourselves.

While World War II was raging through Europe, C. S. Lewis was bolstering people's theology in England on a lecture tour. He was once challenged by a factory worker at one of his lectures on how Christians could support the war effort when they are taught to love their neighbors. Here is how he answered the thorny question, focusing on what it means to love yourself:

> You are told to love your neighbor as yourself. How do you love yourself? When I look into my own mind, I find that I do not love myself by thinking myself a dear old chap or having affectionate feelings. I do not think that I love myself because I am particularly good, but just because I am myself and quite apart from my character. I might detest something which I have done. Nevertheless, I do not cease to love myself. In other words, that definite distinction that Christians make between hating sin and loving the sinner is one that you have been making in your own case since you were born. You dislike what you have done, but you don't cease to love yourself. You may even think that you ought to go to the police and own up and be hanged. Love is not an affectionate feeling, but a steady wish for the loved person's ultimate good as far as it can be obtained.[3]

There is a critical difference between self-renunciation and self-hatred. Self-renunciation is emptying yourself of your rights as Christ did, although He had every right to throw His divine weight around. "He did not consider equality with God something to be grasped, but made Himself nothing, taking the very nature of a servant, being made in human likeness" (Philippians 2:6-7). The starting line of a disciple's life is following the master's example of self-renunciation. Jesus once said to a group of potential candidates, "If anyone wishes to come after Me, he must deny himself, and take up his cross and follow Me" (Matthew 16:24, NASB). We deny ourselves just as He Himself did.

But denying yourself isn't the same as hating yourself. Lewis' point is to disassociate the warm feelings of affection from our definition of love. He defined love as "a steady wish for the loved person's ultimate good." We may not always feel warmly about ourselves, but we can live with a steady wish for our ultimate good. We can always aim to stand back up, brush ourselves off and walk in the light of God again. We can always love ourselves as a choice.

If you don't really love yourself, this whole Gospel of Grace New Testament thing doesn't really work. Going beyond the bounds of self-renunciation brings you to a dark place of self-loathing. It may look humble to writhe around in your sackcloth and ashes, but it's a counterfeit. You simply can't love others if you don't love yourself. If you can't forgive yourself, then you'll have a hard time forgiving others. If you don't distinguish between the sin and the sinner in you, you will hate both the sins and the sinners out there. Let that go for too long and you could end up like one of those obnoxious religious people that you can't stand to be around.

You may meet someone like the fiendish green Grinch, a creature whose heart is "two sizes too small,"[4] and you wonder how that person ever wound up as a "bad banana with a greasy black peel."[5] If you could look into their souls, you would see a lot of self-hatred oozing out. Here is the Grinch talking through his calendar out loud (from the film version as played by Jim Carrey):

> **The Grinch**: The nerve of those Who's, inviting me down there on such short notice! Even if I wanted to go my schedule wouldn't allow it. 4:00, wallow in self-pity; 4:30, stare into the abyss; 5:00, solve world hunger, tell no one; 5:30, jazzercise; 6:30, dinner with me—I can't cancel that again; 7:00, wrestle with my self-loathing...I'm booked. Of course, if I bump the loathing to 9, I could still be done in time to lie in bed, stare at the ceiling and slip slowly into madness. But what would I wear?[6]

Deep down in their downsized hearts all Grinches hate themselves. We were meant for so much more glory than tight-fistedness and self-loathing.

I'm so thankful there is another option of handling the dichotomy between our high values and our low reality, which doesn't involve kicking the other person or beating ourselves up.

The Heartfelt Cry of Desperation

The third orientation toward this dichotomy is called desperation. It's neither settling for lower values nor sinking into despondency because of how you are missing the mark. It's crying out to God from the bottom of your slimy pit, even while loving yourself the whole time. My life may be in shambles and I may have even caused this mess, yet God "brought me out into a spacious place; He rescued me because He delighted in me!" (Psalm 18:19).

Let's go back to the sofa chat when my wife confronted me with how I hadn't been living out our values of emotional intimacy in our marriage. What if I had quelled the shrill little voice within me rising up in self-defense, slaying the ugly monster before it could defend its master? What if I had opened my mind to the Holy Spirit, the one who convicts us of "truth, righteousness and judgment" (John 16:8) and simply let her talk? I didn't do any of this, sad to say, but it would have gone something like this:

"You are right, honey. I have not been meeting your needs for emotional intimacy. I've been checking off the right boxes but not really connecting with you. I do want to be able to slow down and look in your eyes and really listen to you, but I know I haven't been doing that." After making sure she felt fully heard, I would add the shocking kicker, "Will you forgive me?"

Instead of rebuffing her (turning outward) or feeling guilty (turning inward) I would drag my dichotomy to God (turning upward) and cry out to Him, "Help me, God. I'm not being considerate with the way I'm living with my wife. Help me to consider her needs. I confess..." In other words, what if I were to agree with God's standard of "Husbands...be considerate as you live with your wives" (1 Peter 3:7), confess I was falling short of that mark and then desperately cry out to the Father to "be conformed to the likeness of his Son" (Romans 8:29) in my marriage and in all the categories of my life?

I think I would have one happy wife.

Growing desperate is a life value. It's crying out from the slimy pit of your current reality to the One who can set you on a rock of higher values. It's not lowering your values or living with guilt. It's keeping the values exactly where they are and striving to reach them with the grace of God.

How would growing more desperation in your life affect your relationships? What would happen, for example, if the next time someone criticized you, pointing out that you espouse Value X yet you are living out Reality Y, you simply agreed with them. Instead of counter-suing or caving into self-pity, you simply responded that you are guilty as charged. You're absolutely right. I need to work on that. Thank you for pointing that out.

Then afterwards, leaving your gape-jawed friend, shocked spouse or dumbfounded boss behind, you slunk to your prayer closet and cry out to God? What if we were continually desperate for God to make us into the image of His Son? *What if we knew how impossible that was but we tried anyway?*

This might take some practice for those of us who have a lot of frequent Sunday School miles to our credit. We're so used to projecting an image to the world that we have it all together even when our inner world is falling apart. Inside each one of us is the heart of a Pharisee, a friend once told me, and every day we have to engage in mortal combat to defeat that poser.

Let it be publicly proclaimed, we're a mess and we need Jesus.

The Original Facebook

The Scriptures liken themselves to a mirror that a man holds up to his face. James the brother of Jesus used this analogy. As we peer into the Word of God we are immediately stunned by our own glaring imperfections. *Whoa—look at the little piece of spinach between my teeth! And those zits!* But as we gaze deeper in, as we "look intently into the perfect law that gives freedom" (James 1:23-25), and respond with obedience, we will find ourselves *not hating ourselves but loving Him more.* The story line of New Testament life isn't so much our own ability to attain to godly attributes but that we allow our hearts to be stretched out in desperate, clutching love for Him.

A man like that, who "looks intently"—gazes, stares, captures, ponders, meditates—and then follows through with obedience on what he sees "will be blessed in what he does" (James 1:25).

Take some time today to look intently into the original Facebook. It may not offer the instant gratification of social media, but it will reward you with abiding joy if you can slow your soul down long enough to peer in. You may not like what you see as you come face-to-face with your own imperfections, but you will sense the Author's intense love for you. Those moments in the mirror will stir a greater desire in you to seek His perfect face.

The outward orientation smashes the mirror. *Get that thing away from me. Don't remind me. Just back off and I'll be fine.* The inward orientation smashes its own image inside the mirror. *I hate myself. The truest thing about me is that I'm a failure.* The upward orientation has the courage to look into that brutal mirror but then looks straight back up to God. *It's true I'm a mess, Lord, but have mercy! You are bigger than this issue. It's so amazing that You love me! I need You.*

We were wired to be desperate. There is no godly life outside of a fierce grappling with God. My friend and author Paul Richardson writes about how it all begins:

The Creator even arranged your *first breath* as a moment of desperation followed by an encounter with His grace. When you came to consciousness inside your mother's womb, you immediately found yourself submerged in a cramped condition. Your living space was limited but you were warm and well-fed. It is ironic that you now celebrate your birthday. Your birth assaulted you like a jolt of thunder and lightning in the night. There was blinding confusion followed by panic. As you were pulled out of the warmth of your cozy water world into a tempest of light, your lungs suddenly heaved for oxygen, but you couldn't breathe. Your suffocated soul cried out for help and you could do nothing but wait. Then the shadow of the Almighty crossed over your face. He knelt down and breathed life into your nostrils. Your lungs were opened and flooded with oxygen. Your first breath initiated your preordained journey from despair into hope.[7]

Your first breath was a cry of desperation. Every day of your life you are confronted by your failures to achieve the godly values that bring you life and the dreams that God has stirred within you.

Let that dichotomy drive you to Jesus. You didn't get saved by yourself and neither can you attain the life you dream of by your own will power or self-efforts. The good news and the bad news is that we will still need a savior.

Now think on your own couch of conflict, external or internal. What would it look like for you to rise from that complacent ambivalence and embrace a lifestyle of desperation?

Jesus, I feel like a mess and You know that more than anyone. I confess how I have blown it and have not lived up to Your standards for my life, both internally and externally, throughout all my relationships. I choose to agree with my adversary quickly and will not defend myself any longer. I also reject hating myself over this because You treasure me. I confess that improving myself is impossible with my own will power. Thank you that all things are possible with You. I look to You for deliverance and freedom. Jesus, please save me again today.

CHAPTER TWO

THE SPIRITUALLY DESPERATE

I was in Singapore, staying over one night with a short term mission team while in transit back to Texas. Our accommodations in Indonesia had been pretty bare and simple, so we were all looking forward to a good night's sleep in a nice hotel. We were so grateful that the airline had put us up in a nice one before the long journey home. I was most looking forward to the breakfast buffet.

While loading up on bacon and eggs at the buffet, I noticed a slight commotion at the restaurant's entrance. In walked Kofi Annan, who at the time was the Secretary-General of the United Nations. He just walked right in with his official entourage, smiling and waving to people as he made his way to the buffet line. I came back to our table and talked to my teammates in a hush.

"There's Kofi Annan!"

After questions of who's that and where is he, I stated my desire to go over and introduce myself. My friends said go for it, but I suddenly felt reluctant. Kofi was an important man, at that time directing the UN's affairs around the world, and I was just a lowly breakfast gawker. They said, come on Mike, just go over there and say hi, and I finally said nah, devouring my breakfast at an observable distance from the action. I just didn't have a big enough need in my life at that time to require breaking through Kofi's bodyguards and interrupting a very important man as he started his busy and very important day.

Change the storyline. What if at that moment I were a refugee from a chaotic nation ravaged by civil war and ethnic cleansing, believing firmly that the UN was the only hope to save my country from spiraling into bloody oblivion? All other efforts had failed repeatedly. If that were the case, I probably would have torn through the restaurant, ripped through the bodyguards and grabbed on to Kofi's expensive suit. "You have got to help us," I would shout out to him inside the packed restaurant. "You must save my country!" His security detail would have peeled me off Mr. Annan and tossed me outside onto the pavement, warning me that I would be arrested if I tried to re-enter the premises. I wouldn't mind the embarrassment, as long as Kofi heard my plea and it registered with him.

But that morning I just wasn't desperate enough about anything to risk losing my reputation.

One Chance

Once there was a lady who was totally convinced she was an absolute wreck without the touch of Jesus, so much so that she was willing to lose her reputation one dusty day:

As Jesus was on His way, the crowds almost crushed Him. A woman was there who had been subject to bleeding for twelve years, but no one could heal her. She came up behind Him and touched the edge of His cloak, and immediately her bleeding stopped.

"Who touched me?" Jesus asked.

When they all denied it, Peter said, "Master, the people are crowding and pressing against You."

But Jesus said, "Someone touched me; I know that power has gone out from Me."

Then the woman, seeing that she could not go unnoticed, came trembling and fell at His feet. In the presence of all the people, she told why she had touched Him and how she had been instantly healed. Then He said to her, "Daughter, your faith has healed you. Go in peace." (Luke 8:43-47)

Jesus was a busy man, heading toward another important mission to heal someone who had already booked an appointment. But this audacious lady just couldn't take losing another drop of blood from her wrung-out body. She was going to grab hold of this miracle man, no matter the repercussions. Avoiding a frontal assault, she made her move stealthily, creeping up from behind. That way no one could stop her. It's much easier to ask forgiveness than permission, as they say. She was not going to let her chance of healing pass her because of a dinky little thing called personal dignity.

Jesus was moved. Moved so much that He stopped. He focused on her. He sensed her desperation. Her frenzied faith connected with His power and it flew out of Him, like a power cord demanding electricity from a high-voltage outlet.

With her reputation in tatters, she fell at His feet in front of all those gawkers and confessed that it was indeed her. Jesus was impressed. He called her a daughter. He complimented her faith. He blessed her in peace.

To Jesus, there's something so attractive about desperation. It seems to be able to get His attention like nothing else. It stops Him in His tracks. His heart is drawn to the ones without any other options.

Compare her poor-in-spirit response to someone else Jesus met who thought he pretty much had his act together. This wealthy nobleman had lots of options. He was the kind of guy that most of us would envy—an up-and-coming leader, independently wealthy and at least trying to live a godly life.

Yet the Savior honed in on the one area where this non-desperate man was not cutting it, the one area where he needed saving. Before Jesus lowered the boom on this guy, the Bible actually records Jesus' emotions at that precise moment: "Jesus looked at him and loved him" (Mark 10:21). Wow! Jesus felt such affection for this guy who was really trying to live up to godly values. And because Jesus felt this love for him, He couldn't go easy. No pep talk. No "You're doing okay for the most part. Those values you've attained are enough. Keep up the good work." Jesus poked His finger right in the one stronghold of the man's heart. "One thing you lack," Jesus told him. "The money thing.

You just gotta let it go. Give it all up, get risky and generous and you will have a stellar reputation in heaven. Then come, follow me." (my paraphrase)

The man's face dropped and he "went away sad, because he had great wealth" (Mark 10:22).

The point that follows is not that hell will be filled with rich people. Yes, it is true that the love of wealth can clog up the eye of a needle even more than a camel. But the real point of the story comes out in the question that dribbled out of the disciples' dumbfounded mouths, "Who then can be saved?" (Mark 10:26).

They were thinking, "Whoa, this guy seems to be doing pretty good. He's obeying the rules and even seems to be financially blessed. I mean, come on, if *he* can't enter the kingdom of God, who possibly can?"

Then comes the whole point of the story. No one is cutting it. We are all drowning in our sins and shortcomings, none of us being able to save ourselves. Jesus then gave an exclamation point to what they were already thinking: "With man this is impossible." I imagine the master teacher pausing and looking around at His shocked listeners, while a few ticks of awkward silence passed by, before He threw them the lifeline. "But not with God. All things are possible with God" (Mark 10:27).

Even a successful, God-fearing man couldn't get saved by himself. Neither can you. You needed and still need a savior. A main point of the Old Covenant was to show what a mess we are on our own. That hopelessness and failure begs the question, "Who then can be saved?" In one of Paul's illustrations, Old Covenant law is a tutor who guides his student toward graduation day, the freedom of the New Covenant (Galatians 3:24). In another place he put it simply, "Christ is the end of the law so that there may be righteousness for everyone who believes" (Romans 10:4).

Spiritually desperate people get it. All things are not possible with me, not even close. But not with God. All things are possible with Him, even saving a wretch like me.

Friend of the Broken

You're at an informal gathering at a friend's house. You notice a lady you haven't met before sitting on the couch by herself, sipping a red plastic cup of fruit punch. She seems to be avoiding eye contact with the other partygoers and shifts nervously in her seat. Your friend whispers to you quietly, with a tinge of caution in his voice, "She is really needy."

Would you want to occupy the seat next to her on the sofa?

Or you're at a nice restaurant and the hostess is walking you and your longtime friend to your table. You've been looking forward to catching up with him over a hearty meal. On the way, your dinner companion notices someone he recognizes sitting by himself. The somber man is wearing yesterday's fashion and gloomily picking at a salad. Your friend says under his breath before he introduces you, "This guy is really desperate." The sweaty-faced stranger looks up and offers a half-smile.

Now, are you hoping with all your might that the lonely diner is not invited to eat with you?

Desperate people have been called EGR's in some Christian circles—Extra Grace Required. We label and avoid desperate and needy people. They drain us. They take up our time and energy and must be stopped before they leech all the emotional energy out of our souls. Avoid them at all costs.

But Jesus somehow lived His life differently. I think at that party Jesus would plop Himself down on that sofa and have a long heart-to-heart with that broken lady. He would invite that guy eating by himself over to His own table for a life-changing conversation. The great friend of sinners and other dysfunctional riff-raff seemed to be almost drawn like a magnet to desperate people.

Too Broken To Care

Shut up, Blind Bartimaeus, important people are coming through here. Like the desperate woman, this blind man chose freedom over reputation. The miracle man was passing by and old Bartimaeus also wasn't going to let this one opportunity pass him up. Causing a ruckus, he started calling Jesus by His messianic title, "Son of David," and wouldn't let up. Just some crazed lunatic crying out to Jesus.

The raging vagabond's desperation prompted a question in Jesus. "What do you want me to do for you?" (Luke 18:41). Wasn't it obvious already? Somehow getting the man to admit his need was important in Jesus' diagnosis and treatment.

The man was too broken and busted-up to feign contentment in his circumstances. Old Bartimaeus asked for a miracle straight up. He didn't say, "Could you give me patience to continue my life as a blind man, learning patience along the way?" or "Could you help me clean up a little, or at least get a better tin cup?" He got right down to the bone of his need. "I want to see" (Luke 18:41).

Jesus seemed to like the honesty and simplicity of his answer. And in the blink of a new eye, he was healed! Philip Yancey writes in his book *What Good is God?*, "Of all the people healed by Jesus, Bartimaeus is the only one whose name the

Gospels record."[8] Yancey points out that Bartimaeus' name in Hebrew means "son of garbage." This person that humanity had discarded, Jesus honored with a transformative miracle.

Also notably, Blind Bartimaeus was given the same affirmation as the desperate woman: "Your faith has healed you" (Luke 18:42). But wasn't it Jesus' power that healed him? Yes, but the access point to that power was faith birthed out of desperation.

Does this mean God will heal you every time if you're desperate? Is there some sort of guarantee that we have been missing? Maybe you haven't been healed yet because you're not desperate enough? Sometimes I wish God would take some of the mystery out of the universe and give us some straight talk, some formulas that work every time. Like a catchy Sunday school song I once learned:

> I wish I had a little box
> To put my Jesus in
> I'd take Him out and (smooching sound 3x)
> And put Him back again

Make Jesus simple, keep Him in a box and take Him out when I wanted! Wouldn't it be great to have some sort of miracle vending machine—insert desperation and out pops the miracle? We know it doesn't work that way. Life is too messy and complex, with way too much mystery involved. But if Jesus happens to be passing along my dusty street, I'm going to be calling out to Him just like our unpretentious friend Blind Bartimaeus. I know that desperation seems to stop Jesus in His tracks like nothing else.

The Tumble

Mary Forsythe was a successful pharmacy owner in Dallas, Texas, enjoying wealth from wise investments, living a jet-setting life and sipping expensive wines with her cultured boyfriend. She cut some ethical corners in how her pharmacy dispensed government-subsidized antiviral drugs for HIV patients. And she got caught.

Her fascinating book, *A Glimpse of Grace*[9], chronicles her tumble from the pinnacle of success to the bottom rung of incarcerated society. When she first entered the Benton County Jail in Texas, she assumed her higher-up connections would be able to secure a pardon from the White House. A few days before the new inauguration, and thereby her best chance for an official pardon, she wrote in her journal:

> 1/16/93: No matter what the news, I'll be fine. I'm strong; I can handle it.[10]

But the get-out-of-jail free card never came. Over the course of three years her self-confident persona was broken by the harsh reality of prison life and she soon gave up trying to "handle it." She eventually turned to God in humility and He transformed her. Her soul broke free though she remained inside prison. In one journal entry she marvels at the relentless way the Holy Spirit pursued her calloused heart:

> 8/9/95: What a night in the Lord I've had. It is a great moment when the Holy Spirit takes the light of His Word and penetrates your heart. Even though there is pain, there is joy. Even though

there is sadness, there is freedom. The Holy Spirit showed me my heart. It was bad. I wept and asked forgiveness for not walking in love. Something happened tonight.[11]

Mary was used greatly by the Lord in prison to soften the hearts of her fellow inmates. She counseled them in a mop closet, cried with them at chapel services, prayed for them to be delivered from their demons and helped them find the Truth and a dignified future for their lives.

Her ministry bloomed out of a broken heart over her own pride. She no longer felt she was above silly things like needing a Savior. She fell on the rock of Jesus and was broken to pieces, then poured out her broken life to others (Matthew 21:44, Luke 20:18). Since her release, she has traveled the world sharing her remarkable story and bringing hope into many dark places.

Another Mary embraced that same humility when she prayed over 2,000 years before, "I am the Lord's servant. May it be to me as You have said" (Luke 1:38). Mary Forsythe's life was also transformed and set on a remarkable journey after offering up a heart of humility followed by resolute submission.

The Bruised Reeds

Your gut-honest desperation pleases the heart of God more than your religious performance. In the prophecies of the coming Messiah, written hundreds of years before Jesus appeared to fulfill those ancient forecasts, the Christ was painted as not only a fierce warrior king but also a tender-hearted counselor. Isaiah the prophet wrote of this coming King, "A bruised reed He will not break, and a smoldering wick He will not snuff out" (Isaiah 42:3).

In other words, you may have thought that God was going to break the weak, but the opposite is true. The people barely hanging on by their fingernails are the very ones God is going to lift up. He delights in the desperate.

Are you a candidate? Are you in the same category as a foul-smelling beggar or a blood-drained sickly woman? He wants to meet you in whatever your place of desperation.

The poor in spirit are not looking at Jesus as someone who can help them augment their already-successful lives. They are real and open and clutching on to their savior, day after day.

Spiritual Self-Sufficiency

The thing that nauseated Jesus about the Laodicean church wasn't their brazen sin but their spiritual self-sufficiency. The Asia Minor town was an important banking center and had a famous medical center. These were important people doing important things. Life was hopping and they were busy. God helps those who help themselves was probably their motto. Jesus called their spiritual temperature "lukewarm" and called them on their self-sufficiency, living busy lives apart from Him:

> You say, "I am rich; I have acquired wealth and do
> not need a thing." (Revelation 3:18a)

He saw right through their reputable facades into their true heart condition, then rebuked them for being so blind to it:

> But you do not realize that you are wretched,
> pitiful, poor, blind and naked. (Revelation 3:18b)

Harsh words. Not the kind of verse you would see on a refrigerator magnet or in a sappy, Christian-themed greeting card. He wanted to splash cold water in their faces. He wanted them to open their eyes and get desperate: "So be earnest and repent" (Revelation 3:19). In other words, get real. Really real. While you're at it, change your attitude that I am this little rabbit's foot of a friend who helps bring some luck and success to your lives. Before Jesus we all are desperate, whether we see it or not.

Then He offers to connect with them in a true fellowship of the heart.

> Here I am! I stand at the door and knock. If anyone hears My voice and opens the door, I will come in and eat with him, and he with Me. (Revelation 3:20)

This astounding invitation of intimacy, often quoted to non-believers in evangelistic conversations but really meant for the church, comes only after they would turn from their spiritual self-sufficiency and turn to Him in open-hearted honesty. They were required only to get up from their own place of pride and open their front doors, welcoming them into a heart-to-heart conversation with Jesus in the ambience of a dinner setting. Imagine! Eating dinner with the best listener you have ever known, unburdening your soul to this counselor King, one who has all the understanding you crave and all the power you could ever need.

Jesus loves it when you're desperate, when you come to the end of your self-sufficient self. That's where He enters. He is the Savior who delights in saving you, again and again.

Lord, You alone know the full extent of my sin and brokenness. I cry out to You from this wretched place and bare my heart before You. I want to reach out and touch the edge of Your cloak and ask You to turn my way. Jesus, Son of David, have mercy on me! I choose Your freedom over my reputation. I call on You to set me on a rock and to put a new song in my heart. I turn from my pride and I open the door, asking You to save me again. I repent from my self-sufficiency and eagerly confess that I am still in need of Your saving.

CHAPTER THREE

———

THE EMOTIONALLY DESPERATE

We stumbled out of the doctor's office and I felt nauseous enough to fall and crash against the carpeted wall on the way down the professionally decorated corridor. My wife and I weren't speaking to each other yet—our mouths were too dry to speak and no words could be formed to express our pain in that moment. Our hearts were beyond broken by one little word.

Autism.

For months we had been taking our three-year-old son to different specialists while we navigated through what we thought would be a six-month furlough from the mission field.

At age two our second son wasn't speaking that much and we thought maybe it was a bi-cultural issue. He was hearing three languages every day—English, Indonesian and the local dialect of Javanese. Surely he would sort it all out eventually and start speaking. Other friends raising kids cross-culturally told us their children were late talkers, too. No reason to worry.

But months passed and he still wasn't talking much, just a few words here and there. A doctor friend suggested we get his hearing checked and the tests came back as normal—there was nothing wrong with his hearing. We went to other doctors who said he was fine, not to worry.

Yet there were some other things about our little guy that weren't quite right. Giving him a haircut was like taking him to the torture chamber. Kicking and screaming. He had lots of tactile issues. To eat an ice cream cone, he would close his eyes tightly to steel himself. He flapped his arms a lot when excited, scared or happy. He never pointed at anything but would pull us by the hand to the places he wanted to go. Lots of things we saw as unique but we didn't know enough about the autism spectrum to recognize any developmental red flags. All around he just seemed more intense, more difficult, more easily agitated. He also enjoyed strange hobbies, like taking every single book off the bookcase, rifling through each page and then tossing them aside. The saddest part was that he couldn't share with us what was going on in that cute little head of his.

The doctor that morning leaned forward, looked into our worried eyes and uttered the word that had already been hanging in the air the last several weeks. From her mouth it made it sound so much more real, more official more permanent. The word sucked the air out of the room.

Autism.

"Are you still breathing?" she asked us.

We assured her we were but our hearts had stopped beating. She tried to put a brave spin on the diagnosis and told us about lots of hopeful options and about autistic people who went on to lead normal lives, but we really didn't hear any of it. We were devastated.

We made it home and my first call was to our good friends Joel and Courtney who were going through the same challenge of raising a special needs child. They knew well the road from denial to diagnosis. They weren't home and I tried to leave a message on their answering machine, barely able to choke the words out. "We...just...got...the diagnosis..." The tears erupted out of us as I shared the news with the first people we could think of, making our new reality feel very official. Stephanie and I slumped down on the floor and cried together.

Later Joel and Courtney called back. I so appreciated them in that moment. They didn't try to encourage us. They didn't say you can lick this thing. They simply shared their deep sorrow with us over the news and then gave us some great advice. "You guys just need to be sad for a few days and process this," they said. "Don't let anyone try to encourage you. Maybe you guys just need to get out of town for few days and just mourn this."

We took their advice. Making plans quickly, we headed off to San Antonio and went on what we later called our "sad vacation." We got as far away from well-meaning encouragement as we could on a limited budget. We took the kids to attractions like Sea World and filled their little lives with amusement park happiness during the day and Mom and

Dad wallowed low in the dregs of depression at night. We really needed time to mourn the news and it felt so good giving ourselves that permission. Our hearts felt the margin not to be brave little soldiers in the wake of the news. We felt so cared for by our friends, for giving us that space to grieve.

Sometimes life sneaks up behind you like that and does a flying leap kick to the small of your back. *Where did that come from?* Recently I talked to a close friend about a mysterious mass found near his brain stem...more tests needed. The results of those tests will profoundly change his life. What could I say to my friend, facing the possibility of a brain tumor while raising three daughters? Of course I said I would pray, and I do honestly pray for a preemptive miracle. But I also offered to him what our friends offered to us when we were at the bottom of our own pit: comfort. *So sorry you are going through this.*

Deadening Disappointments

Life hasn't turned out the way we planned. The time investment we put in hasn't paid off. The prayer request remains unanswered. The promotion never came through. No matter how many times we have pleaded with them, they still haven't changed. The breakthrough is still way out there somewhere. I'm stuck in this hopeless storyline and my heart has gone bone dry in the heat of life's relentless disappointments.

Life for David hadn't turned out the way he had planned. Here he was, the previously anointed king of Israel, on the run from retiring king Saul. He fled to one kingdom, called Gath, and had to stoop to the level of acting like an insane person to save his skin. The king found out that he really was a mighty warrior and David knew that they were going to kill him for it. So he went on the run again and escaped to the cave of Adullam. There in this dark dungeon it was written, "all those who were in distress or in debt or discontented gathered around him, and he became their leader" (1 Samuel 22:2). The once and future king was hiding out in a moldy cave with 400 mal-contents, not knowing what to do next. This was not going according to his plans.

How did the young king feel right then, right there in his dark, musty cave? I'm so glad the Bible is so gut honest and lets us know exactly how he felt that day. Here is his journal entry from that afternoon:

> A *maskil* of David. When he was in the cave. A prayer.
>
> I cry aloud to the LORD;
> I lift up my voice to the LORD for mercy.
> I pour out my complaint before Him;
> before Him I tell my trouble.
> When my spirit grows faint within me,
> it is You who know my way.
> In the path where I walk
> men have hidden a snare for me.
> Look to my right and see;
> no one is concerned for me.
> I have no refuge;
> no one cares for my life.
> I cry to You, O LORD;
> I say, "You are my refuge,
> my portion in the land of the living."
> Listen to my cry,
> for I am in desperate need. (Psalm 142:1-6)

David took honest assessment of his situation. Those who were pursuing him really were too strong for him. Then he took honest assessment of his heart. "No one is concerned for me," he lamented. (Psalm 142:4).

But he didn't stop there...he poured out that lament to God. And we, too, have biblical permission to be gut honest, to pour out our complaints to God.

Another David, this one with the last name Brainerd, was also good at pouring out his gut-honest soul to God. He served as a missionary to Native American tribes in upstate New York and his 18th century life was full of one setback after another. As a young man he was expelled from Yale University after someone reported him for saying, in a private conversation, that one dean there had "as much grace as a chair." Despite his sincere apologies to the dean, he was expelled.

Though he was described as having "bouts of melancholy" (which today would be diagnosed as clinical depression), he pressed on with his plans to become a missionary to Native American tribes. His father-in-law, Jonathan Edwards, found his journals after David's death from tuberculosis at age 30. The great revivalist was so struck by the desperation for God in his son-in-law's writings that he had them published. These journals have comforted and inspired thousands of people since they were published in the 1700's.

Here's an entry from 1743, when he was living in upstate New York, about 20 miles from Albany in the wilderness, trying in vain to reach out to a Native American tribe at Kaunaumeek:

> **May 18** - My circumstances are such that I have no comfort of any kind, but what I have in God. I live in the most lonesome wilderness; have but one single person to converse with that can speak

English. Most of the talk I hear is either Highland Scotch, or Indian. I have no fellow Christian to whom I may unbosom myself, or lay open my spiritual sorrows; with whom I may take sweet counsel in conversation about heavenly things, and join in social prayer. I live poorly with regard to the comforts of life: most of my diet consists of boiled corn, hasty-pudding, etc. I lodge on a bundle of straw, my labor is hard and extremely difficult, and I have little appearance of success to comfort me. The Indians have no land to live on but what the Dutch people lay claim to; and these threaten to drive them off. They have no regard to the souls of the poor Indians; and by what I can learn, they hate me because I come to preach to them. But that which makes all my difficulties grievous to be borne, is, that *God hides His face from me.*[12]

Just like King David, he is real and doesn't hide exactly how his heart feels in the moment. He pours out his complaint and wrestles with God. He even gives voice to the lies that torment him.

The comfort comes a few days later:

May 20 – Was much perplexed some part of the day, but toward night had some comfortable meditations on Isaiah 40:1, "Comfort ye, comfort ye my people, saith your God," and enjoyed some sweetness in prayer. Afterward my soul rose so far above the deep waters that I dared to rejoice in

God. I saw that there was sufficient matter of consolation in the blessed God.[13]

Both these journals and the Psalms have comforted people across the centuries because they don't sugarcoat life's weary problems. In them we are given the permission to be real with our hearts. We're allowed to lament. We can bring those disappointments to God, pouring out our complaints to Him and asking Him for our heart's healing.

Jesus' Quiet Times Not So Quiet

Perhaps if we visualize Jesus' prayer life, our mind imagines Him kneeling at a large rock in the wilderness, His hands politely clasped in reverent prayer, with His head tilted up slightly as a soft, ethereal light drifts downward. A peaceful time of reflection and solitude.

The real image is much more emotive and raw:

> During the days of Jesus' life on earth, He offered up prayers and petitions with loud cries and tears to the One who could save Him from death, and He was heard because of His reverent submission. (Hebrews 5:7)

Jesus' quiet times weren't all that quiet. I imagine Him pacing in the desert, face straining toward heaven, crying out to God for some soul comfort when His cousin John was murdered. Or maybe there He is stooped under a tree, exhausted after another packed day of healing the masses and badly needing some refreshment from the Father to start it all back up again in a few hours. Crying out to God yet again. Loud cries. *Help, Father.*

Or maybe here He is wrestling with an important decision, like choosing the twelve men who would become His followers, the ones He would pour all of His time and energy into.

> One of those days Jesus went out to a mountainside to pray, and spent the night praying to God. (Luke 6:12)

He spent hours of prayer on that mountain, bringing the names one by one before the Father. It was the last name He had the most trouble with. Even as He sensed that the last slot was destined to Judas Iscariot, He was haunted by the prophecies that hinted at the coming betrayal:

> Even my close friend, whom I trusted, he who shared my bread, has lifted up his heel against me. (Psalm 41:9)

I imagine that was not an easy decision and there were many loud cries heard before heaven's throne that evening. *Father, are you absolutely sure You want Judas as one of my disciples?* We know He knew what Judas would later do. At the Last Supper Jesus asked His disciples rhetorically, "Have I not chosen you, the Twelve? Yet one of you is a devil!' (He meant Judas, the son of Simon Iscariot, who, though one of the Twelve, was later to betray Him)." (Isaiah 6:70-71).

Yet even with foreseeing all this, in painful submission to the Father's will, He chose the future traitor as His follower. On the next day, after that intense, all night prayer session, we read:

> When morning came, He called His disciples to Him and chose twelve of them, whom He also designated apostles: Simon (whom He named Peter), his brother Andrew, James, John, Philip, Bartholomew, Matthew, Thomas, James son of Alphaeus, Simon who was called the Zealot, Judas son of James, and Judas Iscariot, who became a traitor. (Luke 6:12-16)

Notice that Judas Iscariot's name is placed last, where it usually sits on the lists of the twelve disciples. I'm conjecturing here, but perhaps for Jesus accepting this traitor into His inner circle demanded an all-nighter of gut-wrenching, wrestling prayer.

In the Scriptures we get a picture of Jesus, this full-fledged perfect mint image of the character of God, as someone with real, raw emotions. In our paintings He may be that very nice man sitting for His portrait, the one with the feathered bangs and Norwegian blue eyes who wouldn't hurt a fly, but in reality He was a full-feeling, fully-colored, fleshed-out human being.

He also didn't endure His crucifixion in a posture of painless contemplation. At least twice on the cross He cried out "in a loud voice" (Matthew 27:46 & 50). Once we hear Him shout out in despair, "My God, my God, why have You forsaken Me?" (Matthew 27:46, Mark 15:34). The other comes at His dying breath, unimaginable agony culminated with the declaration, "Father, into Your hands I commit My spirit" (Luke 23:46).

What does this have to do with us? If Jesus was 100% real with His emotions, then we have permission to be 100% real with ours. The goal of our spiritual lives isn't to detach our emotions from our reality like a Buddhist monk. We're invited to live out the full spectrum of feelings, from sulky to jubilant.

Good Christian Troopers

I have a generous-hearted friend who started a new church in an affluent suburb with high hopes and vision. After a couple of years, the young fellowship just wasn't growing anymore. It had reached a plateau in every category and there just wasn't enough money to keep renting out the store-front property they were using for office space and for Sunday services. After a difficult round of meetings with the church elders, they all decided to close shop. He then threw himself back into his former profession and kept on going.

I asked him about it at lunch one day. I wanted to know how his heart was coping after the death of his dream.

"I haven't really thought about it that much," he said, his chipper tone surprising me as he chomped on his salad. "I've been so busy getting back into real estate."

What was that? How could he not think about it? He felt called by God to launch out and start this church. He had the word of the Lord. People rallied around him in the vision. All of that down the drain two years later with nothing left but unpaid bills.

As he talked I suspected he had gotten busy to cover up the deep pain of that experience. My fear was that later the disappointment would deaden his soul if he didn't let it air out before God. I gave that counsel to him, in so many words, and he said he would think about what I was saying. I hope he did for the sake of his heart.

He may have felt he was being a good Christian trooper. Life's tough. Get over it. Move on. I can hear a few of you Sunday School star pupils out there saying: *Yeah, I thought we weren't supposed to complain!*

Yes, you're right. We are supposed to be dauntless troopers in this life, not grumblers. The second chapter of Philippians exhorts us:

> Do everything without complaining or arguing, so that you may become blameless and pure, children of God without fault in a crooked and depraved generation, in which you shine like stars in the universe. (Philippians 2:14-15)

We are called to serve (helping a friend fix a flat tire, pay our taxes, take our kids to soccer practice) without rolling our eyes and mumbling under our breath.

I reminded my son of this one day while we trekked on the island of Komodo in Eastern Indonesia with two other father-son pairs. This famous island, teeming with Komodo dragons, was the scene of an unforgettable adventure trip for all of us. It was hot and we were thirsty and tired from all that hiking. My son kept saying, "Dad, I'm hot...I'm thirsty...I'm tired." After a few rounds of murmuring, I told my recently-turned 13-year-old son what I had heard once from a friend about the difference between a boy and man: It's the ability to endure pain.

I got on his case. "Son, I want to see you turn into a man. One mark of a man is his ability to endure pain. When you keep announcing you're uncomfortable, you are constantly reminding all of us that you're still a boy. We're all hot. We're all thirsty. We're all tired. But we're not announcing it every five minutes."

He looked at me with eyes slightly ashamed but I could see a light in him also wanting to rise to the challenge. The message was coming out loud and clear, much more powerfully than if I had simply demanded, "Stop complaining!" I challenged him to a higher level, a standard of manhood. Paul did the same in challenging us to "shine like stars in the universe."

We are not given permission to announce to the world every five minutes how uncomfortable our shoes are. That kind of grumbling is obnoxious.

But at a heart level, in the privacy of your own prayer closet, you can "go there." You can look up to the face of God with a journal open in your lap and rant away in that place of emotional vulnerability. He can handle it. The presence of God is the safest place on this planet.

If you don't do it there, it's going to spurt out somewhere else, either in resentment toward others, or it will seep down into your own heart as a dulling numbness. Just like David eventually came out of that cave, your heart is going to make its way out to the light of day. In what condition is your choice.

Parched Zeal

I could feel that something had died in my heart. Standing before a group of Muslim college students in my living room, at a weekly English club my wife and I led, I would have rather been anywhere else on the planet than right there. The discussion was pleasant, the students seem engaged in the day's topic, yet I just felt so distant, so tired, so bored. Give me a soda, my sofa back and a television show, and get all these people out of my living room. That was kind of how I felt.

As cross-cultural workers to Indonesia, we had been entrusted with the mission to befriend these students and to bring them to Jesus. And we did that happily, for the most part, for four years. We created this English club a place of community for them. They seemed to enjoy coming and every week we sprinkled the seeds of God's word into their hearts by choosing simple stories from the Scriptures. Hopefully they would encounter the love of Jesus in our home, with our family, meeting after meeting, week after week. And even more hopefully, they would want to follow this same Jesus, the same source of this love that motivates our family.

I could remember a time so intent on reaching Muslims with the Gospel. The desire would pour out of me in tears at times. But now, at best, I just was going through the motions. I was leading this English club of university students for all the right reasons but with none of the heart.

Why even bother, a voice taunted me from the inside. *You know how this story ends.*

During a season before, in a different city, there were a different set of faces before me. A living room cram packed with Muslim university students. Laughter. Games. Songs. Lively discussions. An environment of community. Discussing Bible stories in small groups in tight huddles on our living room floor, watching for positive reactions from people who seemed hungry to learn more about this Jesus.

Sardu was one such English club member who seemed particularly open. His eager face and generous smile attested to his desire to learn more about this book we loved so much. We met Sardu as a young man in his late teens working as a janitor for a university, a place his family would never be able to afford for him to attend. But he had a lot of drive anyway and really wanted to learn English on his own. Sometimes he was persecuted by friends in his neighborhood for getting too "uppity" by always carrying around an English-Indonesian dictionary.

Fast forward four years later. Sardu had become almost like a part of our family. He called our youngest son Jordan his little brother and sent us lengthy text messages gushing with emotions about his love for our family. We took him to the mall and got him some nicer clothes to wear for a job interview. We got to know his family. We prayed for his mother when a neighbor put a curse on her and the family's business. We visited him in the hospital. Over the course of all this time, Sardu's heart became more and more open to Jesus.

It was such a sweet evening when he prayed to receive Christ in our home. So genuine. So teary. He stayed up that night and read the first seven chapters of the Gospel of John. I felt like doing summersaults that morning after breakfast when Sardu was telling our family how much he felt a love for of Jesus. This is what it's all about, I thought. This makes all the sacrifice of moving here, along with all the tremendous time investment, totally worth it!

Sardu went back to his house and his life and his family. Word got out that he had turned Christian, although we counseled him to just say simply that he was following Jesus now (and not that he had become one of those immoral pork-eaters). The pressure from his community started building. One day I met with him at a busy food court in Surabaya and I asked him about getting baptized. Was he ready for that kind of declaration of his new found faith?

He replied cryptically, "God hasn't spoken to me about that yet, Pak Mike, so I'm not sure if that is something I should do."

We talked a little about Jesus' command on the subject and then I dug a little deeper. He picked around at his rice and finally came out with the reason. He simply didn't want to disappoint his parents, whom he had already told that he wanted to start following Jesus. "They said that if I ever got baptized, then I would cease to be their son and not bother going to either of their funerals." He's an only child, very close to his parents, and they lean on him financially. The price for him was just too high.

We stayed in touch. We met with him when we visited his city. But every time we talked with him I could sense him distancing himself us from us, and more sadly, from Jesus.

And then came along two more similar stories, two more Muslim college students who embraced Jesus, grew quickly and then withered away.

Seasons later we started an English club in our new city. Standing in front of a fresh group of faces, with a deadened heart, the voice kept taunting me: *you know how this story ends*. All this work, all this time investing in these relationships...and the ones who do come to Christ will eventually just fade away.

Maybe I should just give up and not try to start a new story. These stories just peter out, just trail off somewhere down the chapter in mid-sentence.

I sighed and began the lesson.

After that lifeless English Club, I realized how dead my heart had become. I began getting honest about the deep places of disappointment in my heart and let out before God the deep sighs of grief over the people who had fallen away. I poured out my complaint to Him. I lamented and asked why. I told Him how I didn't feel like going on any more in this vision to see Muslims transformed by the Gospel. I told Him I had had enough. Go on without me.

I felt my words, so potent and honest, were making it all the way to heaven. The God of all comfort began to restore my heart with His tender presence. He brought caring and comforting people to me that prayed for those hurt places. I rested a while with Him before I got up again.

Later more disappointments came and I brought my sad heart to Him again. And He lifted me up...again.

Don't let disappointment deaden your desperation. Remember how much your honest heart cry moves the heart of God. Bring those disillusionments to the One who can restore your heart in the light of His love.

God cares about you and all those disappointments matter to Him. He's not trying to squeeze as much ministry as He can out of you and then toss you aside into the wastebasket. Sometimes He makes you lie down in green pastures, leading you beside quiet waters so that He can restore your soul (Psalm 23:2-3). He delights in tenderly shepherding your hurting heart. He cares for you deeply and intimately, because He really is a good father.

God, I've got to be honest here. I am deeply disappointed with how life has turned out for me. If I may say so, it seems unfair. My hopes were so much higher than the current mess of my reality. I see how that disappointment has deadened my heart. I pour out my complaint in Your safe presence, Father. Before You I tell all my trouble. Listen to my cry, for I am in desperate need. Restore me. Comfort me. Renew me today.

CHAPTER FOUR

———

THE RELATIONALLY DESPERATE

My wife and I are at our first counseling appointment, sitting on opposite ends of a sofa. The room is cold from a potent AC, its hum the only sound in the awkward silence. The emotional temperature is even icier. Our counselor Jim, whom we have just met for the first time, is scribbling something on his legal pad.

He looks up to study us, perhaps to jot down some flash of insight. We steal a glance at each other but there is little flicker of hope in our deadened eyes.

How did we find ourselves here, in this cold counseling office? I know very well the "presenting problem" that caused us to schedule our first appointment, of course: our frequent and sometimes intense conflict. The angry words ripping through the air of our home, again and again. It was getting so bad that our young children were complaining about it. Their hearts were not feeling safe at home, hearing mommy and daddy argue so much. We opened up about this to our pastor, who said forget about pretending to be the perfect Christian couple and go get yourselves some help. I know this urgent pain very well, but over the long run how did our relationship disintegrate to this point? How did we go from intimate allies to merely cordial roommates and then disintegrate to warring factions?

Jim asks if we will open up and share some of our most frequently occurring conflicts. There are plenty to pick from.

After some exhibits are laid on the table, I clear my throat and tell him how I *really* felt about Stephanie and accuse her of all manner of selfishness. She feels deeply hurt to be dishonored like that in front of a professional stranger and then her emotions quickly turn to anger over getting ambushed. Unfortunately for her our session was up before she could share her side.

The drive home was even colder and quieter than the counselor's office. "So that's how you really feel about me," was the only thing she said as she stared dead ahead on the road. "Thanks."

Heaven's Side of the Story

Now imagine this same scene through a window of heaven. Jesus is watching two of His beloved sit far apart on a sofa in a counselor's office. He knows they have been living even further apart emotionally, and His heart moves toward them in grief. After all, He created these two, knows them better than they know themselves and has loved them even before they were both born. Not only that, He endured an excruciating death to deliver them, not only from the punishment for their sins, but also to detangle their hearts from selfishness and move them toward freedom. He desires that their hearts thrive in a healthy, intimate relationship.

Yet those hearts have grown cold toward each other and anger is seeping through, spilling over and scaring their own children with insecurity. His children.

"What God joined together, let no man separate," Jesus once said to a group of religious contrarians who were looking for technical justifications for their own hard-heartedness. He doesn't take too kindly to covenant breaking and here's the full reason in context:

> "Haven't you read," He replied, "that at the beginning the Creator 'made them male and female,' and said, 'For this reason a man will leave his father and mother and be united to his wife, and the two will become one flesh?' So they are no longer two, but one. Therefore what God has joined together, let man not separate."

> "Why then," they asked, "did Moses command that a man give his wife a certificate of divorce and send her away?"

> Jesus replied, "Moses permitted you to divorce your wives because your hearts were hard. But it was not this way from the beginning." (Matthew 19:4-8)

But it was not this way from the beginning. Before the first couple walked the earth, God intended marriage to be a place that cured our aloneness. This sacred relationship between a man and a woman would be a safe place of emotional, physical and spiritual intimacy. We still feel that original intention in our hearts and that's why it hurts so badly when it breaks down.

We all know deep down that it's not good for us to be alone, yet the magnetic poles of our heart seem to drive us toward separation and isolation. Why is this? *Because your hearts were hard.* Our own stubbornness and refusal to repent keeps us not only in rebellion against God and His original design, but also mired in self-centered isolation from one another. I imagine Jesus making this statement with a deep sigh. The New Covenant is all about us getting a new, soft heart; when they callous and harden over, He is grieved.

Not only does the breaking up of what He has joined together make God grieve but apparently it also makes Him mad. What He has sanctified and joined together is serious business in heaven and its shattering arouses His anger. Here's how He feels about marriage covenants being broken, once again by pious people who are great at playing religious games but missing the point on the matters that are most important to Him:

> Another thing you do: You flood the LORD's altar with tears. You weep and wail because He no longer looks with favor on your offerings or accepts them with pleasure from your hands. You ask, "Why?" It is because the LORD is the witness between you and the wife of your youth. You have been unfaithful to her, though she is your partner, the wife of your marriage covenant…So be on your guard, and do not be unfaithful to the wife of your

youth. "The man who hates and divorces his wife," says the LORD, the God of Israel, "does violence to the one he should protect," says the LORD Almighty. So be on your guard, and do not be unfaithful. (Malachi 2:13-16)

I hate divorce. Now that is a potent and potentially offensive statement. God actually links it to violence because of its destructiveness. We all know people stumbling out of the wreckage of divorce and have witnessed its soul-wrecking collateral damage. Chances are that's your own story. God's heart is always to protect His beloved, and His anger is aroused toward anything that causes that much damage (*anything*, not anyone). Marriage was to be a special place that not only satisfies our lonely souls but also brings life and protection to the world. Its destruction "does violence to the one he should protect." (Malachi 2:16).

God is one. In His very being, as seen in the essence of the Trinity, there is relationship. His heart always beats toward reconciliation and relationship.

But Stephanie and I weren't feeling any of that in the cold counseling office that day. The angels may have been rooting for us but we didn't hear them. Honestly we didn't consider heaven's thoughts on the matter at all. We were thinking what most of us feel in disintegrating relationships: why I'm right and he/she is wrong.

Heaven Back In Your Picture

What if the next time you came to a relational stalemate, you brought God into the picture? You looked toward heaven and simply asked, "Lord, how do You feel about this?" Maybe we don't want to do that, because we sense that God is never going to say, "You know, I totally agree with you...he/she really is being totally selfish here!" We know better and that's why we don't ask.

This is where hard heartedness begins, the refusal to bring our small "r" reality to God's big "R" REALITY. How does someone go from "until death do us part" at his or her wedding day to "maybe I married the wrong person" or "God just wants me to be happy" a few short years later? Hard heartedness, left un-repented, slowly kills soft heart tissue and metastasizes into deep-rooted lies.

Relational Rescue

We did make it to the other side. During our next session, our seasoned counselor gave my wife the opportunity to share things from her side (and we all know there are *always* two sides). Tears flowed, forgiveness was offered and received, and our stalemate began to thaw. Over the next sessions and at a marriage retreat with other couples, he helped us to see the unmet needs under the surface that were driving our conflicts. He shored up our theology on marriage, explaining that though Adam had the perfect relationship with God and sin had not yet entered the world, there was still an ache of aloneness in his soul. Even with a close relationship with God, we will still have relational needs...those aren't going away anytime soon. He got us to see that those emotional needs are valid and that we were uniquely equipped to meet those needs in God's mysterious and wonderful design. He walked us through several healthy marriage principles that we had been ignoring for a long time.

At our next session we were sitting closer together on the sofa and even dared to hold hands. At the last session we were practically snuggling on that sofa and had nearly forgotten about the cold AC.

God broke through and heaven smiled.

I'm glad to say it stuck. We've had ups and downs since then, of course, but the trajectory of our marriage has been toward closeness. At the time of this writing, we have been married for 24 years and I can honestly say our love is deeper and stronger than ever.

Before you ask me for the contact information of that amazing marriage counselor, I want you to think of the main player in this story.[14] Jim may have been the best supporting actor but God was the director. Marriage is His idea, His design and His heart, even when I'm not feeing it. I may feel hopeless, or my wife may feel our relationship is lifeless, but that is never God's intention.

There is more to marriage than just trying on our own to apply helpful principles to our hurting relationships. Beyond our own bad decisions and against the enemy who tries to rip us off, God is always contending for our hearts. "The thief comes to kill, steal and destroy," Jesus said, "but I have come to bring abundant life" (John 10:10). God's heart bursts full of life and hope, from eternity past, during every second of every day, and on into forever. That abundant life that He exudes is intended for every category of our lives, especially in our most important relationships. If we really believe this marriage stuff is His idea, we will feel that same holy fight for marriage rising up in us.

Hope Crusted Over

I remember being on a trip once and visiting with a friend who was leaving his wife. This is someone who was such an inspiration to Stephanie and I earlier in our spiritually formative years, when we all lived in the same city. Now, years later, he was sitting on his sofa, explaining to me the justification for following a heart that was deceiving him. It felt like the *Invasion of the Body Snatchers* to me—the person looked the same but it was someone else's soul talking. He used to be so full of heaven's purpose and joy, but in this conversation I didn't hear him bring heaven's perspective into the picture at all. What in the hell (literally) happened? Some lie from that pit seeped out, he agreed with it, and it devastated his life, his wife's and their children's. I left sad and dismayed.

Imagine how heaven felt.

I've talked to other friends lately who are divorcing. Their love, once deeply rooted and rich, has dried up and died for complicated and complex reasons. I've been able to have some heart to heart talks with them and tried to be a good listener, trying to offer some comfort and truth. In the course of each of these conversations, they seem to always want to move the topic back toward what a rotten, horrible, selfish person their spouse is. Collaborating evidence is frequently brought out to validate their accusations. Even a quick phone call to them ends up with a replay of the recent ills of their spouse's incorrigible wretchedness.

Go back to the morning of their wedding day. They woke up so full of hope. Giddy with anticipation and joy. On that blissful dawn, none of them would have ever predicted their relationship, so full of life and romance and longing for each other, would evaporate and be replaced with cold bitterness and seething resentment. At one point during their courtship, they couldn't help going on and on about the glorified wonder of their fiancée. Now they can't help going on and on about the sinful selfishness of their soon to be ex-spouse.

Isn't the same Jesus who joined them together on their wedding day powerful enough to resolve the current relational crisis? We only have to give heaven a chance. Jesus is willing to meet us more than halfway...He already proved that to us once.

Relational Caveat

Please don't take me wrong if you are in a harmful or untrue relationship. I realize there are some boundaries that should never be crossed, including physical abuse, and that Jesus did give an exception for marital unfaithfulness. Working toward reconciliation in those awful situations is an excruciatingly hard process, and I don't want to heap on any more hopelessness on you than you already feel.

In his excellent and challenging book, *Sacred Marriage,* Gary Thomas makes a powerful argument that hanging in there, even in a tough marriage, can reap huge spiritual benefits in our lives. But at the same time, he also cautions to treat people who can't summon the energy to salvage a hurting relationship with much understanding and grace:

> Anyone who has been married for any length of time should be able to understand how truly difficult marriage can be, and how, even among Christians, tensions can rise so high and hurt can be so deeply embedded that reconciliation would take more energy than either partner could ever

imagine possessing in ten lifetimes. In many cases, God can and will provide the energy; in some cases, people are just not willing to receive it. Before a divorce is final, I'm usually going to encourage someone to hang in there, to push on through the pain, and to try to grow in it and through it. Happiness may well be beyond them, but spiritual maturity isn't— and I value character far above any emotional disposition. With heaven as a future hope, spiritual growth as a present reality, and, in many cases, children for whom our sacrifice is necessary, an intact marriage is an ideal worth fighting for. But that doesn't mean we should treat those whose marriages have crumbled as second-class Christians. Jesus spoke of high ideals and absolutes—but He loved real people with acceptance and grace.[15]

As with Gary's target audience, I'm also speaking more to those in salvageable relationships, people who are reading marriage books because the luster has been lost in their relationships but not beyond miracle-saving power. To the broken-hearted, the stalemated, the separated, the lonely, the married older folks who have lost each other along the way—the relationally desperate—I want you to see God's heart for reconciliation in this well-known and powerful truth:

Therefore, if anyone is in Christ, the new creation has come: The old has gone, the new is here! All this is from God, who reconciled us to

Himself through Christ and gave us the ministry
of reconciliation. (2 Corinthians 5:17-18)

All this is from God. His miracle-working, new creation
power works in and through us for reconciliation.

Miserable Fakes

God gives grace to the humble (James 4:6). Pointing fingers
and growing colder may be easier, but humility is the
prerequisite for His miracle-working reconciliation. Growing
desperate is the only way forward. An intimate marriage will
remain elusive for those of us who are non-desperate, or at least
good at playing the poser.

Especially for those of us in ministry, the professionally-
paid Christians, posing is always the strong temptation. We're
supposed to have our act together, after all, and when we don't
we may lose the respect of the people we are trying to lead.
Better to suffer in silence (usually until there is a public melt
down).

"Ministry couples are the worst," our marriage counselor
once told me. "They get really good at playing pretend and after
a long time forget how to be real with their hearts and to be
vulnerable with other people."

He spoke of leading an intensive marriage retreat with four
couples. The three ministry couples plastered smiles over their
hurting hearts, but among the small group was a used car
salesman (really) and his wife. The two of them felt no such need
to pretend. They came in hurting and weren't afraid to let all
their pain hang out. The ministry couples feigned that they
wanted to learn some really neat principles to bring back to their

churches to minister to hurting marriages, yet behind-the-scenes their own relationships were in tatters.

Through the course of the four-day marriage retreat, the used car couple led the way in vulnerability. They experienced the greater breakthrough because as we know, God always gives grace to the humble. Thankfully their example helped the ministry couples come out from behind their white picket fences of ministry and bring their hurting relationships to the light. God worked powerfully in their hearts and relationships as well.

Why is it so hard for saved people to get saved? We've gotten too good at playing religion and need to get back to this core value of desperation. That heart attitude of humility is like a set of landing lights for God to come in and work His miracles.

Can we grow desperate, getting gut-honest and grace attractive before it's too late?

Rediscovery

I remember one morning taking my cute little newborn daughter to breakfast at the deliciously Southern restaurant *The Cracker Barrel* so the rest of the family could sleep in on a Saturday. As I was there, spoon feeding grits to my Indonesia-born daughter (to make sure she understands that deep down she's still a Southerner), I looked around the busy restaurant. There were so many older couples eating their hearty breakfasts in complete silence. A quiet man would take in one fork full after another of morning chow while reading his newspaper. His seemingly lonely wife would take a sip of coffee and stare out of the window into the parking lot, both of them in dead silence. At table after table, over the course of a full hour, it looked like there were more biscuits and gravy consumed than words shared at the packed restaurant. You can see scenes like that of older lonely couples and think, yikes, is isolation that inevitable? The older you get, the less you pursue each other? Are those my choices? Bitter divorce or lifeless coexistence?

No way. No way. No way. Jesus died for so much more than that.

The Last Stand

Recently I had lunch with a good friend who is going through a bad divorce. His wife is the one who is making the decision to walk out and he's totally broken and bitter over this for understandable reasons. I realize there are two sides to every story and, by his own admission, there are some boneheaded things he did to bring his marriage to the brink.

My friend is wanting to hang on and work through it and she's had enough and wanting to walk out. This man loves Jesus and wants to pastor his children through this awful season. My heart breaks for him and I have tried to offer comfort. Yet I did give him this challenge toward the end of our lunch, "At the end of time, will you be able to look Jesus in the eye at the Judgment Seat of Christ and honestly say that you did everything in your power to save your marriage?"

He cried a little at that question and admitted no, he hadn't done everything in his power to reconcile. He said the strongest feeling he has toward his wife is anger. Understandably, there has been no fight inside him toward reconciliation based on his wife's decision and response. The context of this conversation is that we are good friends and can shoot straight with each other. I wouldn't say this to just anyone, but I did remind him of the verse, "If it is possible, as far as it depends on you, live at peace with everyone" (Romans 12:18). As far as it depends on you, I urged him, do everything in your power to make peace.

Months later, as I was working on this section in a public place, he walked by and we had a follow-up conversation (I love these "coincidences").

"Hey, Mike," he said with a gleam of determination in his eye, "I'm going to ask her."

I knew what he meant, ask her if she would be willing to give their marriage a second shot, to be open to the process of reconciliation.

Wow and whoa. I was blown away. I said, "Man, I can't imagine how hard it would be for you to open yourself to that kind of deep rejection again. I so admire your courage."

"Pray for me," he said as he walked away. "I believe reconciliation is always God's heart."

That is a potent statement from a man who has lived through hell and yet is still contending for heaven. *I believe reconciliation is always God's heart.*

Are you living inside a hopeless-feeling marriage? I feel for you. Yet I encourage you to look deep down under that pile of relentless disappointments and crushed expectations. Can you hear the faint heartbeat of God's purposes and desires for that relationship, for your selfish spouse? For selfish you?

Is it too late for you? There is a real reason you felt so attracted to him during courtship days. There were many reasons. Guys, you couldn't get her out of your head and you bored your friends to exasperation with her praises. The thrill from courtship and honeymoon days may seem like a very long time ago, but I'm convinced that love can be rekindled and passion can grow richer, sweeter and deeper. Guys, go find her again. Ladies, that dashing man is still there, somewhere.

The creator God, the one who is continually making all things new, wants to restore your desperate marriage. It may feel like a black hole to you right now, but He can transform it into a source of life for you again. I want to see you one day at The Cracker Barrel, years from now, holding trembling hands, sharing your golden hearts with each other and gazing into each other's eyes until your dentures fall out into your biscuits and gravy (or feel free to paint your own picture of a preferred future for your relationship).

Marriage is hard work, seemingly impossibly hard. It's hard enough with Jesus trying to soften two hard-hearted people, I can't even imagine trying to do it without Him! But because He is in my marriage, and believing that it's His idea, and that His desire is that it's a place of glowing warmth and rich intimacy, I have hope. Bring heaven's hope into your warped picture. Choose to call out to the God of relational hope, again and again.

Lord, You know that it's not good for me to be alone, but I feel so alone in my marriage. You've joined us together to cure that aloneness, yet I feel so much separates us. Help me to rediscover the wonder of my spouse. Open my eyes to see all the ways my needs are being met through my spouse and help me respond with a heart of gratitude. I release my judgments and repent of my selfishness. I need Your grace in being more proactive to meet my spouse's valid needs and to make time for our relationship. Make our marriage a place of life. Rekindle it with Your love again. Restore us, God. Thank You that You make all things new.

CHAPTER FIVE

DESPERATE FOR COMMUNITY

I was a fidgeting five-year-old, attending a special program at our local Baptist church. On the pew next to me sat my big sister and on the other side our neighborhood friend Russell. We stared ahead at the churchy proceedings, and I asked Russell what the tank of water was behind the stage.

Russell was wiser and older (nine), and I often looked to him for advice. He explained that the tank of water was where people got baptized. I wasn't a regular churchgoer yet, but I had heard that word before.

"How do people get baptized?" I asked him.

Russell pointed at the ornate, red velvet chairs that were placed beside the pulpit on the stage, facing toward the congregation. "You see those chairs?" he asked.

"Yep." They looked like thrones to me.

"When someone feels like they are old enough to get baptized, they run really fast from the back of the church down the aisle, jump up on one of those chairs and try to fly all the way over the choir loft and into the water tank. If they make it, they are baptized."

Wow! Suddenly I wasn't feeling bored in church anymore. "What happens if they don't make it?" I asked.

"Then they aren't old enough to be baptized and they have to try again later," Russell explained.

Okay then. I looked around at the congregation, mostly older folks, and figured they had already made their run long ago. I scanned the crowd for the younger people and wondered who would try out their wings tonight. It would take a lot of guts to try to clear the banister of that choir loft but I couldn't wait to see someone try.

As the church service wore on, most people just sat there and listened passively to the pastor drone on and on. I kept glancing back at the back of the church, but no one was even warming up for their takeoff, not even during the altar call. I started wondering if Russell was telling the truth, especially after I noticed my sister once shooting him a mean look. Maybe he was just pulling my leg, but what if he wasn't? That would be so cool to see. I kept an eye out just in case.

To my disappointment no one lifted off that night. I quickly learned that churches are predictable places. After accepting Jesus at a camp that the church sponsored, I got baptized the old fashioned way and never got a chance to clear the choir loft.

I am so grateful for the church life I experienced in my childhood because I really met Jesus there. But most of us would agree there is a difference between the predictable experience of how we organize our Christianity today and what we read on the Bible's pages: the controversial and miracle-working Jesus, along with His risk-taking and kingdom advancing early followers.

Think on God's original intention for the church, this body of believers that Christ would lead with His kingly authority and fill with His abundant life:

> And God placed all things under His feet and appointed Him to be head over everything for the church, which is His body, the fullness of Him who fills everything in every way. (Ephesians 1:22-23)

Whatever the church is, it should be a place where the fullness of Jesus fills every dimension in every way. The disappointment and angst that gnaws in us about our own faith communities points to the yearning for God's original design.

Recently I was speaking to my single friend, I'll call him Charles, who shared with me the gnawing ache of loneliness that he often feels in church community. This is supposed to be the place that fills him up and deeply connects him to God and other people, yet he can't shake the disappointment of that not happening. I asked him if he wouldn't mind writing about that yearning for authentic community, and he sent me back an email. "My experience with Christian community has been marked by a few pleasant memories of seasons of precious community experiences," he began, "surrounded by long periods of drought and dissatisfaction." Charles touched on the different seasons of his life, beginning with when he gave his life to Christ and enjoyed rich community. From there he moved to different cities, taking leadership roles in different ministries as he pursued his career. He always appreciated the warmth he felt inside these Christian communities, yet a darker side of his life, entangled in sexual addictions based out of a bruised past, never seemed to break through to the surface. He longed to find freedom within the context of these communities that were pursuing Jesus together. He talked about his experience in one community, a house fellowship that was more organic and Spirit-led than tightly organized:

> Occasionally, people would share about some struggle in their life and we would pray for them or prophesy over them as the Spirit led. Of course, as is usually the case, most of these struggles were with the world around us (i.e., pray for my children, pray for my job, pray for my upcoming surgery) rather than the deeper type of struggle within us. During those meetings, it felt as if the Spirit of God filled all of the emptiness within me. After I left the meetings, however, that feeling of emptiness and loneliness would return, sometimes before I even made it to my car.[16]

After a few more moves and in and out of different church communities, Charles finally joined a sexual addictions recovery group where he is still fighting toward freedom. He now attends both a traditional church along with these more gut-honest meetings. Disappointment lingers that both groups can't seem to be one in the same. Charles summed up his regular fellowship experience with, "I met some really nice people at church who seemed genuinely interested in getting to know God but did not seem nearly as interested in getting to know me."

Loneliness. Disappointment. Frustration. *Why isn't this deeper? Why are we so shallow? Why aren't we going someplace together and changing this world?* Charles' heart is yearning for something in church life that you are yearning for, too. God designed the Church, this place that is supposed to overflow with the life of Jesus, to go deep in authentic community and wide in world-changing outreach.

That's why you can tend to get more frustrated with your church community than your dysfunctional work environment. Your workplace is probably a mess because it's driven by earth's values and you sort of accept that. But your church? That's the place that is supposed to be contending for heaven's values. You look around at the current reality of your church and something in you knows it was meant to be so much more.

Believe it or not, the world is longing for it too:

> For the creation waits in eager expectation for the children of God to be revealed. (Romans 8:19, NASB)

God has set eternity in the hearts of everyone He ever created, according to King Solomon (Ecclesiastes 3:11). We all have this yearning for a higher reality than the one we are experiencing, toward something transcendent, something *other*. This is why epic fantasy books and science fiction movies sell so well. We were wired to experience something more transcendent than our daily, grinding reality. C. S. Lewis put it this way in his brilliant little book *Mere Christianity:*

If we find ourselves with a desire that nothing in this world can satisfy, the most probable explanation is that we were made for another world.[17]

Add a little suffering into our lives and that yearning only grows:

> For we know that the whole creation groans and suffers the pains of childbirth together until now. (Romans 8:22, NASB)

All of us, believer or non-believer, yearn for the true church to emerge, the children of God revealing His glory in vibrant ways. A place with the give and take of real relationships, where people are known, loved unconditionally and still challenged to live out heaven's values and on mission together. The most hardened atheist in your city would take notice if that became your faith community.

In this chapter I want to focus on closing the gap between the safe and predictable way we experience our Christianity versus becoming an authentic and missional community that pursues Jesus together with desperation and passion. First we'll go deep and then we'll go wide.

Transparency

What keeps our communities as deep as a casual chat in the church foyer? The problem, as my friend and mentor Mark Buckner explains, is that we have competing needs: the need to be loved and the need to be respected. It feels like I have to choose one or the other. If people really know me, I won't be respected anymore. But if I opt for respect and don't vulnerably share my true self, I won't really feel loved. In fact, I will keep feeling unknown and lonely. I compromise at showing my cards enough to feel loved but not too much for fear of losing respect. We're paralyzed in the pincer grip between these two warring needs and most of us opt to keep it safe and shallow in our relationships.

Gary Smalley writes about five levels of communication, ranging from the shallowest to the most meaningful. The first level is the arena of clichés, which he defines as "typical, routine, oft repeated comments, questions and answers given out of habit and with no real forethought or genuine intent."[18] Those are the how-are-you's in the church foyer and the what-a-cute-outfit's at the woman's Bible study. The second level is the arena of facts, which is sharing of information that also requires no in-depth thinking or feeling. Conversation with other believers can easily stay mired in these first two basic levels. It feels safe and friendly but it doesn't go anywhere near the deep needs of our hearts.

Venturing into the deeper levels requires risk taking. The third level he lists as sharing opinions (in which people may oppose yours, like politics), the fourth is sharing feelings (which hits closer to home and heart) and finally the most vulnerable level is sharing needs (which requires a lot of trust in a relationship).

What percent of your own conversations stays in the shallow waters of reciting clichés or disseminating facts? What would it look like for you to venture into these deeper levels of communication? We typically don't "open up" because we haven't taken the time to build trust with other believers because transparency costs us something, a little piece of our reputations.

I was eating breakfast at a busy café in Austin, Texas, with five men in a deep-hearted discussion group and we were all taking turns answering the day's question, "In what area of your life are you being the most passive?"

Even with the loud chatter and clanking dishes around us, it wasn't hard to think of so many areas in my life where I was being passive. But if I were really honest, what would these guys think of me?

Everyone else was opening up and it made it easier for me to lay down my cards when it came my turn. "I would have to say spiritually. I rarely initiate times of prayer with my wife and almost never lead family devotions. On that front I am just missing in action."

Everyone around the table listened attentively as I continued, "I mean in public, behind a pulpit I can wax eloquent and appear very passionate spiritually, but at home I'm just as passive as could be."

"Wow, Mike," said one friend. "That surprises me. I would have thought that you were leading your family spiritually."

One of the other members tried to comfort me. "Well, Mike, you've been very busy, and I think we can all relate."

"Hey, don't go easy on him here," the first friend cut in. "We've got him squirming on the altar here, and we need to thrust the sword through."

I'm so grateful for the tip of that sword in my life. For the last few years, whether I have lived in the U.S. or in Southeast Asia, I've walked closely with a group of allies that I can be completely real with. Usually we have a long breakfast once a week or get together over lunch. We celebrate victories, confess failures and get gut-honest about the real issues of our lives. Sometimes that can be painful, but it has been a place of tremendous life to me.

Usually we don't want to share the ugly stuff but that's the very place where we find the beauty. The Scriptures push us toward confessing our sins to one another and exposing them in the light of safe relationships:

> But if we walk in the light, as He is in the light, we have fellowship with one another, and the blood of Jesus, His Son, purifies us from all sin. (1 John 1:7)

A small, trusted circle of friends can become a safe place for you in overcoming besetting sins. I want to encourage you to do that and go there, but don't stop there. More than just pulling each other out of ditches, we need to inspire each other to run on mountain ridges. As much as we need safe places to come clean with weaknesses, the end goal is holiness and advancing God's calling of our lives. "As iron sharpens iron, so one man sharpens another" (Proverbs 27:17). The end result of the sharpening is a sword useful and deadly in the battle for the life of our community.

Are you walking alone in the battle, far from any true heart comrades? Who would you call right now if you were alone and tempted by an old addiction? When is the last time you came clean with a trusted ally? I remember when a new guy came to this group, we would always ask as an initiation question, "Do you go deep in your friendships with other men?"

The answer was always the same. *No.*

I used to think just men crowded the shallow end of the pool when it comes to relationships but I've heard that our more relational, feminine counterparts aren't swimming in the deep end either. I once put this question to Janine Parrish, a pastor and missionary who has a few decades of experience with women and community. In her view women typically don't go that deep. It's hard to get them together, for one thing. There are so many reasons to keep them apart—the kids and their homework and the driving complications and all the errands. Who has time for a heart-to-heart chat?

Male cave dweller or female errand runner, all of us need to grow in this. Maybe it's time for you to open up a little more. I heard this analogy at a "Wild at Heart" boot camp in Colorado led by John Eldredge. Who would parachute into Normandy on D-Day all by himself and take on the Nazis? That's beyond crazy. The first thing those paratroopers did when they landed off target and behind enemy lines during the dead of night was to use little clickers that sounded like crickets to find their company. No way they were they going to hide in trees and shoot at Nazis by themselves. You need a platoon of men to walk with in the battle of your life because you are toast without them. Don't brush this aside with a *yeah, yeah, heard that before*, but rather embrace the humility to admit you are walking alone and you are losing in this battle. Your enemy "prowls around like a roaring lion looking for someone to devour" (1 Peter 5:8). That's some*one*, as in one man walking alone behind enemy lines. Seriously, make this a priority! Seek out a group of trusted allies. It will require some forethought, proactivity and courage, but the joy of freedom and the comradeship of real community will be richly worth it.

Purpose

I double majored in psychology and journalism in college and one of my most interesting psychology classes was one called "group processes." We studied stages of group development and team dynamics but by far the most unforgettable part for me was a two-hour weekly lab led by a couple of grad students.

For our first lab, 12 of us gathered inside a mysterious room lined with one-way mirrors in the psychology building. There were no chairs but lots of comfortable pillows and beanbags on the floor. A grad student introduced himself and said he would be staying in the room with us during the course of the semester, while his partner would be behind the glass watching us and taking notes. Kind of creepy right off the bat.

The goal of the group was that there was no goal. We were there to process how the group was processing and nothing else. The only rule was that you weren't able to talk about things happening outside the room but only things happening in the "here and now." You could share your feelings in what was being discussed, for instance, but you couldn't make a plan to do something outside that room.

After that brief orientation, the first lab began. I remembered it started something like this:

Grad Student One: "Okay, then, who would like to start the group?"

Student One: "Um, what do you mean?"

Grad Student One: "I mean, who would like to start the group?"

Blink. Blink. Sideways stares in awkward silence.

Student Two: "Maybe we could get each other's names?"

Grad Student: "Okay, that's a great idea. Who would like to go first?"

Student One, "Well, my name is Brenda..."

And so on. My first impression was that this was going to be an extremely long two hours every Thursday night.

But we did get to know each other, very well in fact. After all, we were with each other for two hours a week throughout the semester and had dissected each other's feelings to bits. The grad student purposely led this group passively, only interfering if we talked about anything outside the "here and now." For example:

Student Three: "Sometimes I feel like this lab is an incredible waste of time! I'm so busy and could be doing my other homework right now!"

Grad Student: "I see. How do the rest of you feel about that?"

Student Four: "Well, maybe we should be more positive and give it a chance."

And so on. After the last mandatory meeting, we never really saw each other again. Why? Our community had no purpose, other than processing each other's feelings. We weren't trying to advance any cause, solve any problem or support each other in any larger struggle. We were in it just for us.

Does that sound like your community, warm mutual support but yet with no real mission? I sure hope not. The deepest community I have ever experienced has been with people who were fighting for something bigger than their collective selves, a cause worth dying for together. Think of the camaraderie that develops in the trenches of warfare. Those veterans usually struggle to find that same level of battle-tested friendship again in their lives.

I've seen this dynamic over and over as teams go on short-term mission trips. They come back loaded with fun memories, inside jokes and the long, lingering joy of giving themselves to something bigger than their own lives and personal agendas.

Your community simply has to be *on mission* if you want to feel the richness of camaraderie. It requires a war. The good news/bad news is that we're already in one. We are meant to be the lovesick bride of Christ in the middle of a warzone. Here's Peter spelling out that purpose as a community, drawing from God's call to Moses three months into the Exodus:

> But you are a chosen people, a royal priesthood, a holy nation, God's special possession, that you may declare the praises of Him who called you out of darkness into His wonderful light. (1 Peter 2:9-10, NASB)

This passage is bursting with purpose. Read it again, but this time try to read the "you" as it was meant to be, in plural. We individualistic Westerners tend to read the plural "you" in Scripture as singular, as in "How neat...I am a holy nation!" Read it out loud as if it were coming from the mouth of a general to his army arrayed for battle:

> But you are a chosen people, a royal priesthood, a holy nation, God's special possession, that you may declare the praises of Him who called you out of darkness into His wonderful light. (1 Peter 2:9-10)

Make the purpose of your community God's original purpose: a group of mercy-drenched people proclaiming the excellencies of Him who has called all of you out of darkness and into His marvelous light. I promise you the deep feeling of community and connectedness that your heart longs for will be a delightful by-product. You'll be shoulder to shoulder with deep, battle-tested comrades, forging lifelong friendships. I can't think of anything more fun than doing kingdom adventures with these marvelous comrades.

The Real Thing

Are you desperate for real, authentic community? You're so tired of shallow chit-chat, longing for something raw and real. You've been playing it safe and your community has been walking around in circles inside its own sub-culture. No wonder you're so bored.

Go Deep. Open up. Share your true heart with a group of comrades. Bring yourself to the light and experience an intimacy of friendship that you've never dreamed of. "But if we walk in the light, as He is in the light, we have fellowship with one another..." (1 John 1:7). The Greek word for fellowship, *koinōnia*, is deep, rich stuff. It literally means to "become a sharer."

Go wide. Get on mission. Fling yourself into the bigger picture, into God's bigger story, and you will experience a battle-tested camaraderie that your adventure-hungry heart longs for.

The fight for authentic and missional community won't be easy, but remember that Church was God's idea. Desperately cry out to Him for that deeper, riskier *koinōnia* experience that illuminates the world with His marvelous light.

Father, forgive me for setting the bar so low in my community. I have not opened up and shared my true self and struggles with the ones You have called me to walk with. I choose to walk in accountability. Weave me into true community so that I can walk my life out in the light. I need Your courage in this and I thank You for the gift of true fellowship. As a community we have entrenched ourselves inside a safe sub-culture and have not been on mission. Forgive us, Father. Thank You for Your commitment to our unity in Your purposes together. Build Your church through us.

PART II

———

FOR THEM

...I will appoint You as a covenant to the people,
As a light to the nations, to open blind eyes,
to bring out prisoners from the dungeon
and those who dwell in darkness from the prison.
— Isaiah 42:6-7

CHAPTER SIX

INTENTIONAL DESPERATION

Joe Banks wills his weary body back into his dreary office for another day at the medical prosthetics company where he has worked for over four years. The fluorescent bulbs buzz with a steady hum and dimly light the small group of lifeless employees below. Grey industrial shelving lines the walls and the clicking of a typewriter clacks through the stale air. His boss, Mr. Waturi, is on the phone arguing with someone. DeDe, the secretary whom he secretly has a crush on, offers a perfunctory greeting.

Today Joe has something with him, a cardboard box that holds a bright Hawaiian lamp with a hula girl holding up a colorful lampshade. He turns on the lamp inside his closet-turned-office and stares at the bright dancing lamp wistfully.

DeDe the secretary enters the room as Joe removes a broken shoe from his foot.

JOE: Good morning, DeDe.

DEDE: Hi, Joe. What's with the shoe?

JOE: I'm losing my sole.

"Yeah," she answers absently and then hands him some labels and tells him each one gets sent five catalogs. Joe says he can't do it because he only has twelve catalogs. She exits as he puts his shoe back on. Mr. Waturi soon charges in.

WATURI: How you doin', Joe?

JOE: Well, I'm not feeling very good, Mr. Waturi.

Mr. Waturi chuckles.

WATURI: So what else is new? You never feel good.

JOE: Yeah. Well. That's the problem. Anyway, I got the doctor's appointment today.

WATURI: Another doctor's appointment?

JOE: Yeah.

WATURI: Listen, Joe. What's this DeDe tells me about the catalogs?

JOE: I've only got twelve.

The two of them get into an argument, with Joe defending himself lamely and Mr. Waturi browbeating his junior employee into submission to his strange logic. Mr. Waturi blasts Joe for his shortcomings and lack of leadership.

WATURI: You're inflexible. Totally. And this doctor's appointment! You're always going to the doctor!

JOE: I don't feel good.

WATURI: So what! Do you think I feel good? Nobody feels good. After childhood, it's a fact of life. I feel rotten. So what? I don't let it bother me. I don't let it interfere with my job.

JOE: What do you want from me, Mr. Waturi?

WATURI: You're like a child. What's this lamp for? Isn't there enough light in here?

JOE: These fluorescent lights affect me. They make me feel blotchy, puffy. I thought this light would...

WATURI: Get rid of the light. This isn't your bedroom; this is an office. Maybe if you start treating this like a job instead of some kind of welfare hospital, you'd shape up. And I want those catalogs.

JOE: Then please order them.

WATURI: Watch yourself, Joe. Think about what I've said. You've gotta get yourself into a flexible frame or you're no place.

Waturi starts to leave but stops and looks back.

WATURI: Take that light off your desk.

JOE: I will.

WATURI: Take it off now.

Joe unplugs the light and reluctantly takes it off his desk.

Joe Banks, played to dreary perfection by Tom Hanks in the 1990 film, *Joe Versus the Volcano*[19], is like many of us, resigned to our fates, tiptoeing around confrontation, having dreams of some far away sunny place but taking the colorful lamp of our dreams off our desk. He doesn't have the guts to pursue the girl (played by Meg Ryan) and we don't have the guts to take even a daytrip outside our comfort zones. We are stuck in neutral inside our grueling reality and somewhere along the way, like Joe, we have lost our souls, living out our lives in quiet desperation.

Permanent Brain Cloud

What does risk-taking look like? What would happen if I stood up to the unreasonable demands of my boss, or visited my co-worker in the next cubicle to start up a conversation about spiritual matters? What would happen if I pursued my teenage daughter's heart or confessed this besetting sin to my close comrade? What if I did join the sports league like I've thought about doing for the last couple of years? What would happen if I volunteered time, mixed it up with the lost, went out of my way to do something risky? What would happen if I *engaged* the world around me?

I don't have time for that. Even if I tried, I would be rejected. It wouldn't make a difference anyway.

Those are the lies that Mr. Waturi whispers to us. *Take that light off your desk.* What used to excite us, engage our hearts and captivate our imaginations now seems overly idealistic, almost childish, like that Hawaiian lamp inside of a grey cubicle. But something radical happened to Joe, something that made the hypochondriac the good kind of desperate. It was enough to totally change his life, to the point of him taking on a smoking volcano.

Joe made his appointment that day where he was informed by the doctor that he had "permanent brain cloud," a black fog of tissue running down the center of his brain. The doctor said it was a rare disease, very destructive and incurable, and he was given six months to live.

Joe is stunned, of course, and immediately starts thinking about how he will live the remaining months of his life, which the doctor assures him would be full of "perfect health" right up until the moment his brain and body would suddenly fail.

In the next scene we see him coming back to his office after the three-hour absence, a gleam in his eye and a fight in his voice.

WATURI: What's the matter with you?

JOE: Brain cloud.

WATURI: What?

JOE: Never mind. Listen, Mr. Waturi. Frank. I quit.

Joe packs up the things from his desk, including three books—*Romeo and Juliet, Robinson Crusoe* and *The Odyssey*—while he continues to argue with Waturi. He laments his deep regret for working in the office for four and a half years and Waturi counters that he won't give Joe a reference.

Joe walks towards the front door and stops at DeDe's desk. He looks at her and she stops typing. "Four years. If only I had them now, like gold in my hand. Here, this is for you." He gives her the lamp.

Mr. Waturi insults him some more as he brings his few belongings to the front entrance. "You'll get your check," Waturi sneers. "And, I promise you, you'll be easy to replace!"

Joe pauses and mumbles out loud, "I should say something..."

Then he lets Mr. Waturi have it. He rails about how pathetic Mr. Waturi looks and how the zombie lights suck the juice out of his eyeballs. He rues the horrible tasting coffee and the pathetically low pay. Finally he confesses out loud his regret for not having the courage to make a move for DeDe.

JOE: And why, I ask myself, why have I put up with you? I can't imagine but I know. Fear...

Joe lets a few more choice words fly and says he will not physically harm Mr. Waturi because, "I'm gonna leave you here, Mister Waturi, and what could be worse than that?"

Joe opens the door and leaves. Mr. Waturi and DeDe are frozen. The door reopens and Joe comes halfway back in.

JOE: DeDe?

DEDE: Yeah?

JOE: How 'bout dinner tonight?

DEDE: Yeah, uh, okay.

Joe smiles for the first time since we've met him and closes the door again.

DEDE: Wow. What a change.

WATURI: Who does he think he is?

Mr. Waturi's question goes to the core of our heart's predicament between fear and faith. *Who does he think he is?* Who do you think that you are? Are you a two-bit character in a minor story? Or are you the hero of a great adventure, an epic worth living out? Are you engaging and taking risks to change your environment, or does it have the upper hand and you can merely react to it?

How do we go from the average Joe cowering in our fears to the daring adventurer ready to tackle towering volcanoes? How do we go from risk-aversion to bring-it-on? Can we really live out a life of desperation *on purpose*?

Joe received the precious gift of perspective, a jolting reality check that redirected the course of his life. The doctor's diagnosis helped him see beyond the dingy walls of his closet-turned-office and into the possibility of living in a larger story. The great "what if's" (standing up to Mr. Waturi, asking DeDe out) were suddenly exposed on the shortened timeline of his life.

You and I are living on a shortened timeline. Like Joe, we first need the doctor's diagnosis. A permanent brain cloud is killing us. It's robbing us of the joy that lies beyond the dimly lit room we've cowered inside. It's called fear.

Then we need the doctor's treatment. Our great physician promises that all the risks we take for Him will be worth it. A life lived out in love with Him, in full abandon for His purposes, greatly pleases Him. The smile on His face at the finish line of our lives will be worth any struggle, inconvenience or even suffering we may have endured as we pursued Him and His purposes.

God has audacious dreams for this world. When you're living out the storyline of God's humongous calling for your life, you will become desperate by default. Volcanoes, not managing the catalog collection inside a closet-turned-office, will be your life's challenges.

If your life seems sort of boring and maybe a little bit non-consequential, maybe it's because you're stuck in the wrong plot. You've made the story all about you and that is tediously boring. Your things. Your bank account. Your car. Your lawn. Your Tuesday night fantasy stamp-swapping group. It's just not a big enough adventure to live in.

If you're not desperate right now, then your values are probably too low. Orient your story toward God and other people. Making your life about *Him* and *Them* will jam-pack your life with meaning by default. He invites you to live a life of desperation for desperate people. The stakes will get higher, the risks greater and the adventure more exciting. There will be more warfare because you will arouse the enemy's ire. Fling yourself into that larger story and you'll simply need God more. I'm talking about getting desperate on purpose.

People of Impact

Somewhere along the way in church history, being a good Christian has come to mean someone who is faithful at attending a lot of meetings. As I was growing up, Christians went to church on Sunday morning, good Christians went to church on Sunday night, too, and the really good, hard-core ones added on Wednesday evenings for prayer meetings. The basic formula was the more meetings, the more spiritual. Don't get me wrong, there is nothing wrong with meetings, but the kingdom of God is more about movement. From heaven's perspective, it's more about affecting change in needy and broken people than gunning for the perfect Sunday School class attendance pin.

When John heard from prison what Christ was doing, he sent his disciples to ask Him, "Are You the one who was to come, or should we expect someone else?"

Jesus replied, "Go back and report to John what you hear and see: The blind receive sight, the lame walk, those who have leprosy are cured, the deaf hear, the dead are raised, and the good news is preached to the poor" (Matthew 11:2-5).

Church was never supposed to be limited to safe activities inside comfortable buildings. It was meant to be a force of change in the community, a group of imperfect people who are touching the blind, the lame, the outcasts, the deaf, the spiritually dead and the poor. Its purpose is to swirl through clusters of broken and desperate people and unleash rivers of hope.

The kingdom of God is not a comfortable lounge for well-manicured, pampered princes. It's not for wimpy reeds swayed by gentle breezes. Jesus used this imagery to talk about forceful men like John the Baptist who unleash the movement of the kingdom, then affirmed His cousin's intense temperament:

> I tell you the truth: Among those born of women there has not risen anyone greater than John the Baptist; yet he who is least in the kingdom of heaven is greater than he. From the days of John

the Baptist until now, the kingdom of heaven has been forcefully advancing, and forceful men lay hold of it. (Matthew 11:11-12)

The kingdom is a forcefully advancing clash of violence. It lives in ongoing mortal conflict with the kingdom of darkness. Rough-around-the-edges characters like John the Baptist get it, men and women of action whose lives were marked by passion and not passivity. It's so forceful that not even the very gates of hell can stop its advance (Matthew 16:18). Jesus is looking for forcefully advancing volunteers, risk takers who would join Him in a radical movement that rescues and redeems those captured and enslaved inside hellish prisons.

I know some modern day Joes taking on lava-spewing volcanoes. They are living lives of desperation on purpose.

I love reading their books, like Floyd McClung's *Living on the Devil's Doorstep.*[20] He and his wife Sally ministered to drugged out hippies along the heroin trail that ran through Afghanistan in the 70's and then moved to Amsterdam and started a community-changing drug outreach there right in the middle of the infamous red light district. He raised his family right on the devil's doorstep. Not only did they have impact but they thrived. For their third act they moved to South Africa and started a thriving ministry there.

I love having dinner conversations with people of that caliber. I remember when three young single friends of ours moved to Papua, the easternmost and least developed island of Indonesia. After eight months of language study these three 20-somethings opened up a home for broken street kids in Papua. They took eight-year-olds hooked on sniffing glue and gas fumes into their house. They loved these tough little guys, providing shelter, structure and consistency. Sometimes they were repaid with the kids stealing their belongings, but they kept on loving them anyway. When we had a chance to have dinner with them (taco night was what they usually requested, missing Mexican food), my family would sit there spellbound and could listen to their stories for hours. Nothing on television even comes close to those tales.

I love reading the letters and emails of intentionally desperate people. I've been hearing from a friend of mine in Austin, Texas, who is organizing a ministry to the female workers of men's strip clubs. She does creative outreaches to them, brings treats for their families during the holidays and tries to befriend them. She's also now trying to think through how she can offer new job skills to help rescue them from a degrading industry.

These people are rocking the world with the love of Jesus and I find them downright inspiring.

In 1966, a young lady from England named Jackie Pullinger moved to the notorious "Walled City" of Hong Kong, a place that was so crime-ridden and drug infested that the police hesitated to enter it. The government eventually tore it down, but when Jackie came there the darkened city was ruled by a ferocious drug gang who guarded its lucrative heroin market and prostitution rings. Her riveting story about that experience, *Chasing the Dragon*,[21] captures the grit and the claustrophobic atmosphere of the Walled City but also celebrates the triumph of God's love overcoming the worst ills of society. She simply loved people, tried to help rescue them out of their addictions and prayed almost constantly as she walked the tight alley streets that were forever hidden from the sun. Sometimes the addicts misunderstood her intentions and some even tore up and desecrated the rehabilitation center she built for them. Others found freedom from addiction and prostitution. Her book has been a best seller for over 30 years and she's now one of the most honored citizens of Hong Kong.

I read Jackie's book in college, over 25 years ago and I can still remember the fire that it lit in me. Don't you feel the same around people who are advancing the kingdom in tough places? Who would you rather sit by on a long plane ride, a self-absorbed ego junkie or a Jackie Pullinger? Me too.

There is something else I've noticed about these inspiring people, whether I have known them personally or just admired them from afar. They have plenty of frustration in their life, but it's not self-focused frustration. It's not disappointment that they haven't landed that long sought-for promotion or a mid-life angst. It's the frustration of not seeing greater kingdom breakthroughs in their worlds. They are beating their heads against the wall of kingdom angst. Hearing them lament their longing for greater kingdom breakthrough, more than personal disappointments, is quite refreshing for me.

There's nothing wrong with career advancement, hobbies and personal projects, of course, but I just find people who are all tangled up in other people's messed up lives just more fascinating.

What do people around you hear you most complain about? That you aren't advancing enough or that the kingdom isn't advancing enough?

Turning Toward Them

We've been talking about bringing your own desperation to God for personal transformation. We'll continue to do that, knowing full well what a mess we are, but we're not going to stop there. We're trusting Jesus with all that, as a work in progress, and we're now focusing on loving others well and transforming this broken world. Are you ready?

Jesus was tired. He had been walking for miles and teaching thousands of people, many of whom pushed and shoved their way toward Him to beg for just one touch of healing. It was hot and He was exhausted. Then came the news that His cousin had been murdered by the whim of a cruel despot. He badly needed some alone time up in the hills to find comfort for His soul in His father's love.

> When Jesus heard what had happened, He withdrew by boat privately to a solitary place. (Matthew 14:13).

But desperate people sniffed Him out and spotted Him making His getaway. They weren't aware of His emotional state and probably didn't care. They just wanted their needs met.

> Hearing of this, the crowds followed Him on foot from the towns. When Jesus landed and saw a large crowd, He had compassion on them and healed their sick. (Matthew 14:14)

After caring for their sick and teaching them for days on end, He was also concerned for their pressing physical needs. He thought this would be a good teachable moment for His small band of followers.

As evening approached, the disciples came to Him and said, "This is a remote place, and it's already getting late. Send the crowds away, so they can go to the villages and buy themselves some food."

Jesus replied, "They do not need to go away. You give them something to eat." (Matthew 14:15-16)

The little thought bubbles over their heads announced, "Have you lost your mind, Jesus? Okay, 5,000 heads of families have already pilfered their picnic baskets and all of them are on the verge of fainting from hunger. Don't get us wrong, Lord. It's great to heal sick people and all, but it's really no use if they die from hunger right afterwards, plus we don't see any Super Walmart's out here in these hills, Lord."

"We have here only five loaves of bread and two fish," they answered. (Matthew 14:17)

In other words, we poor fisher folk are so limited against such great need. That's just what Jesus wanted them to realize, that it would be impossible for them to do anything of consequence on their own.

"Bring them here to Me," He said. (Matthew 14:18)

They did and He worked His miracle magic.

And He directed the people to sit down on the grass. Taking the five loaves and the two fish and looking up to heaven, He gave thanks and broke the loaves. Then He gave them to the disciples, and the disciples gave them to the people. They all ate and were satisfied, and the disciples picked up twelve basketfuls of broken pieces that were left over. (Matthew 14:18-20)

A life of impact all starts with the directive of Jesus: *Bring them here to Me.* Limited You comes to Unlimited Jesus and He multiplies your meager efforts to touch the masses. It's easy to feel discouraged about how little our work counts in the grand scheme of things, until we look into the heart of Jesus and see Him stretch His miracle hands out to the desperately hurting world.

An intentional life of desperation. Bring your life, as weak and meager as you feel, to the outstretched hands of Jesus. He's waiting for your loaves and fishes. See that gleam in His eye? He has something special in mind.

Father, I confess I have made the story all about me. The stakes have been too low and the fight too inconsequential. Free me from my own self-absorption and release me into Your great adventure. Open my eyes to see desperate people around me. Give me the boldness to approach them and the tenacity to love them despite their faults. Multiply all my meager efforts to touch them through Your hands, a hundred times over. Unleash me into Your great adventure, making my life all about You and the people around me that You so love. Even though I am still a work in progress, Lord, I ask that You send me out with Your transforming love.

CHAPTER SEVEN

THE POOR

"We are totally out of money," my wife tersely informed me on the phone. "We have to get milk. I'm driving up to the church and we are going to talk about this right now."

The phone call came as I was in the middle of preparing for an outreach at the University of Texas campus. In those days I was leading our church's discipleship training school, which focused on reaching UT with a group of freshly graduated ministry interns, plus working at a regular job part-time. Times were tight and the checkbook balance was lean. Stephanie and I raised some support for this ministry venture but between that and my part-time paycheck, there were holes. Big ones. We tried to live frugally, prayed a lot and took a few trips to the pawn shop to make it month to month. Having a newborn baby, as cute as he was, added to our financial burdens.

Oh God. The priority of getting ready for the campus outreach dissolved into a puddle of urgent prayers for an immediate financial miracle. I found an unoccupied office at the church, got down on my knees and cried out to God. The checking account had twelve dollars, the car had a fourth of a tank of gas, the cupboards were sparse and the baby probably needed a new pair of shoes. You get the picture.

"God, I want to serve You in this vision but we can't go on living like this. You have to provide for us," I pleaded.

As I was finishing that impromptu prayer session, a thought passed through my mind to check my mail slot above the receptionist desk. I had checked earlier in the morning when I came into the church office and there was nothing. But I acted on the impulse and my surprised little hand felt an envelope inside that mail slot. Quickly retrieving it, I tore open the envelope to find an unexpected check for $200! Just minutes earlier I had been dreading Stephanie's arrival, imagining her distraught face, and now I was looking forward to delivering the exciting and amazingly timely news. I had heard before that God is "never late but seldom early," and this definitely proved it. Stephanie entered the church office, our firstborn on her hip, and I excitedly waved the envelope in front of her. "Look, God provided! We just got a check for two hundred dollars!"

Amazed as I was at the timing, we rejoiced together. She drove to the bank, deposited the check and then filled up the car with gasoline and our sparse cupboards with groceries.

"I'm sorry I ever doubted," I told God as I went back downstairs and rejoined the group that was preparing for our campus outreach that day. I related my hot-off-the-press testimony to them, we rejoiced together and I walked on to campus that day with an extra bounce of faith in my step.

Years later I pulled that dramatic story out of my memory cabinet for a sermon illustration when we first moved to

Indonesia. I remember standing in front of a wide-eyed congregation while my missionary friend was translating my first sermon on this island that we had just made our home. At my mentor's suggestion I kept the message pretty general and stayed away from convoluted, sermonic points and sub-points. He recommended beforehand to just tell lots of stories around a few Scriptures. So I prepped a simple message on how we can always count on God to come through for us.

Moving into a section about faith and finances, I told powerful stories from the Bible of how God always provides for His people, tacking on our own dramatic tale of the $200 check. My friend was clipping along in his translation and everything felt so far so good.

"So," I told the Indonesian church that evening, "No matter how desperate you become, no matter if you only have twelve dollars to your name, a quarter tank of gas and you need groceries, God can come through!"

The Indonesians sitting in the pews that evening didn't look very impressed at my story. They just had these polite, glazed looks on their faces. Maybe they didn't understand it? My missionary friend had lived there for many years and I was sure he was doing a good job of translating.

A few at the Sunday night service grunted an obligatory Amen, but I was expecting some heartfelt Hallelujahs to my dramatic story. Come on people, we were at the end of our rope and God came through! But they just stared back at me, as if to say, is there more to the story?

I couldn't figure out why there was no real punch in that testimony but I kept plowing ahead.

After I had lived in Indonesia for several years, I thought back and realized why my inaugural sermon that evening fell so flat. Financial desperation for the mass majority of Indonesians is daily life. Half of them live on less than two U.S. dollars a day and 32 million of them live in abject poverty. In Indonesia, having a car automatically makes you an economic heavyweight. Someone once explained to me the three economic classes there: car = upper class, motorcycle = middle class, bicycle = lower class. The math is pretty simple and most stay mired at the bottom.

So when I said I had *only* twelve dollars and *only* a quarter tank of gas, they were thinking, "Not bad...I wish I had twelve dollars." For most of my listeners that was about a week's salary. They were thinking how nice it would be to have their own cars...what a luxury! They had as much empathy for me as you would hearing a CEO talk about how painful it was to sell one of his corporate Lear Jets because fourth quarter sales weren't as strong as originally forecast.

Base Camp of Gratitude

An American like me who grew up in a comfortable middle class stratum is not qualified to talk about financial desperation because honestly I've never really been there. I'm probably like you, in the 25% of the world that spends 75% of the world's income. I meet people in the developing world who are trying to figure out how to come up with the money to feed their families and I'm sitting on my comfortable sofa inside my air conditioned house praying, *Lord, please, provide enough money so I can replace the broken screen on my iPhone.*

But having had the privilege of living right next to extreme poverty from my comfortable middle class perch has given me a permanent case of perspective. My family and I have squeezed through some tight financial times, but there is no comparison to the masses of people slogging through developing world poverty.

I'm not making the point that you should feel guilty for having so much but rather pointing you to the healthy perspective of gratitude. We Westerners should marvel at all the blessings that rain down on our preoccupied and comparison-prone heads. Get outside your suburb and take a walk on the downside sometimes—it will do your heart grateful wonders.

Typically we compare ourselves to the Jones's extra half-bathroom house down the street. If you're going to compare, it's much wiser to do it downwards. If you are living above the poverty line of food, lodging and shelter, erupt in gleeful gratefulness. Paul wrote to his disciple Timothy that if he had food and clothing, he would be content with that (1 Timothy 6:8). He didn't even add shelter to his basic necessity list! Maybe as a tentmaker, he could always make a tent? Paul felt satisfied on a level of sustenance that most of us would find reprehensible, yet his heart overflowed with gratitude.

So as we talk about moving toward financially desperate people, let's begin with an attitude extreme of gratitude. You may be deep in the valley of debt right now, or maybe staring up the mountain of a financial challenge. I'm just saying let your base camp be gratitude. The average per capita income in the world is $5,600 to $8,300 per year, depending on the method used to determine the number. Let's be generous and round it up to a yearly salary of $9,000. Chances are you are blowing way past that annual sum. Remove your fast food fry cook hat and bow in grateful adoration to your generous Provider.

Cheap Burning Motivations

When you first venture into their world, you will quickly feel overwhelmed and you'll want to draw on some type of motivation to keep going. There are some dirty burning fuels out there, inexpensive and readily available, but if you choose them as your primary motivation, you'll burn out quickly.

Assuaging Guilt. Trying to rid yourself of some materialistic guilt is not enough for long haul motivation. *Look at these wretched poor people! How can we drive these nice cars when they have to walk everywhere? How can we eat in nice restaurants when they barely have enough to eat?* That kind of motivation is a counterfeit for true gratitude, plus it typically doesn't last very long. Maybe after feeling that tinge of guilt you may toss a few coins in the Salvation Army kettle during an annual shopping spree or give a buck to someone holding a cardboard sign. But it's not sustainable for the long haul, because human compassion is a very low octane fuel.

It's the same principle in garnering the motivation to do evangelism. We can feel bad that lost people are going to hell, but it's not really going to motivate us to change our day-to-day lifestyles in the long run. Some of us may even get revved up enough after an evangelism seminar to do a drive-by witnessing to the next lost person we see, but soon afterwards our evangelators will be stuck in neutral again. Feeling bad for other people might make us feel guilty temporarily, but it's not going to ever free us from our tendency to be completely self-absorbed in our own lives. After that initial sting of guilt fades, we just change the channel and go our way. Guilt may make you shift a little on your comfortable sofa, but it's never going to lift you out of your inertia.

Expecting Positive Feedback. Serving the poor sounds very romantic until you spend a lot of time around poor people. Some of them can be lazy, manipulative and sinful just like all of us can. After getting burned a few times, it's easy to keep a stiff arm distance from poor people and judge them as too lazy to help themselves.

I've been lied to, manipulated and stolen from as I've served the poor. I remember being with a shell-shocked short term team on a disaster relief trip when the innocent disaster victims overran our supplies table and grabbed all they could get, hurting us in the process. Those bruised short termers could think, *Well, if that's the thanks I get, then forget it. I'm never doing that again!*

If you are serving the poor because you are waiting to get positive feedback from them, you are going to be disappointed. I've talked to many relief workers frustrated that while they worked hard in the hot sun to build houses for people displaced by some cataclysmic natural disaster, the people they were serving were just sitting under the shade and passively watching. It infuriated them. So forget about basking in a Mother Theresa glow as grateful poor people swarm around you for thankful group hugs. Warm fuzzies falter quickly, I promise you.

Clean Burning Fuel

The poor and needy are…how do I put this…very needy. Ever read Jesus' Parable of the Sheep and the Goats (Matthew 25:31-46)? The hungry, the thirsty, strangers, the sick and prisoners are all featured prominently in it—those are some needy folks. They can drain us. It feels like we can get swallowed alive by all their needs and then leave feeling guilty for not doing enough. Their lives are complicated. We don't always know the right thing to do. That's why the poor are so easy to avoid—we seldom run in to them unless we are intentional. But let's say we are determined to make an impact in the lives of the poor and we are willing to fight through all these complexities and complications. We're going to need a lasting motivation, one based on more than the stirring up of human compassion.

The only pure and clean burning fuel I know of for this mission is Jesus' heart for the poor. This is all from Him and through Him. His heart and compassion will motivate us more strongly than any guilt-fueled efforts at altruism we muster up on our own. Getting thanked or recognized will be nice but it won't be absolutely necessary. Our commitment will be rooted in His compassion, so we must start with His heart. We can continually plug into that power source, no matter how much our emotions may wane. We may even feel nothing and we can be honest with that, too. "Lord, I don't feel like getting into the complexities of poor people's lives. But I know You love them and want to lift them. Please infuse me with Your desire for them."

Let's peer into Jesus' heart for a bit and tap into His desires. He seemed to have a special heart for desperate ones. Here He is quoting Isaiah as He inaugurated His own ministry to a crowd of shocked Synagogue goers in His hometown:

> The Spirit of the Lord is on Me,
> because He has anointed Me
> to proclaim good news to the poor.
> He has sent Me to proclaim freedom for the
> prisoners and recovery of sight for the blind,
> to set the oppressed free,

to proclaim the year of the Lord's favor. (Luke 14:18-19)

Good news to the poor! That's still Jesus' mission today. When we involve ourselves in serving the poor we can't help but feel Jesus' affection for them inside of us. He already knows their story and has loved them from eternity past. When our stories intersect with theirs, we feel a small measure of His heart toward them. It may be just a tiny dose compared to His feelings, but at least that glimmer is enough to keep going.

I've got a group of friends who are leading a vibrant outreach to a lower income, government subsidized housing project in our city. They provide tutoring for kids, lead fun Bible clubs, organize outings and dive into deep friendships week in and week out. I brought my daughter there last week for a block party and the place was buzzing with music, games, balloons, fun and laughter. That outreach has brought so much life to our church. Recently I was talking to a friend who is heavily invested there and I asked her what her greatest joy in ministry was.

"That's easy," she said with a twinkle in her eye. "If I could do anything I wanted, I would quit everything else I'm doing and focus on our outreach full time."

This is someone who is not serving these lower income kids out of a sense of obligation, but rather her mission is fueled by God's heart. Sharing good news with people who don't get it that often—this team feels Jesus' joy in that.

Desperate, Clinging Faith

Faith and poverty share the same definition: a lack of options. Jesus' heart moves toward humble hearts who have no other choices but to cry out to Him. The blind beggar named Bartimaeus wasn't thinking about his 401(k) options when Jesus visited his hometown of Jericho. Jesus was walking by, this was his one chance, and Bartimaeus was not going to let Jesus pass by without making a ruckus first.

I think that's why people closer to the poverty line seem more open to the Gospel. Think of the lady you would meet on a mission trip in a slum, living in constant desperation and hungry for a breakthrough, versus the man living in a comfortable house at the end of a long, tree-lined driveway. He may be miserable, and even admit that, but he's not desperate.

"Blessed are the poor in spirit," Jesus said, "for theirs is the kingdom of heaven" (Matthew 5:3). Remember...this is destitute poor, not working class poor!

Poverty and faith both say I can't do this on my own...I need help. It's the opposite response of the rich young ruler, unwilling to bow down and squeeze through the eye of the needle (Mark 10:17-27). It's more like the response of the hemorrhaging women, reaching out and grabbing the edge of His robe. That kind of humility stops Jesus in His tracks.

Self-sufficiency repulses Jesus and humility attracts Him. These poor ones are already in touch with how needy they are and Jesus' heart is drawn to them in their desperation. He delights to bring them good news and He delights to do that through you.

False Dichotomy

"I don't believe in no social gospel," a Sunday School teacher once told me when I was speaking to his class about our work in Indonesia. I got what he was trying to say, that that we can't just help people practically and not also call them to repentance and to the cross of Christ. Agreed. But beware of a subtle false dichotomy, that you have to choose between spiritual and social transformation. I believe Jesus loves the world enough to send us into theirs, both to redeem broken souls and to restore their broken environments. The cool thing is that you really can do both and each one seems to strengthen the other, mixing soul and community redemption together.

At a recent conference I heard about how some brave saints are responding to a refugee crisis, offering basic food and shelter along with eternal words of truth and hope. It's a both/and, wonderfully resplendent in God's heart.

In Indonesia we started a graphic design outsourcing business with the purpose of lifting people out of poverty.[22] From a two-story rental house in a poor neighborhood and in rented computer labs in local colleges, we offered free computer classes to the community. Hundreds of people learned life-changing job skills through these classes. Some of the graduates joined our team of full-time employees. These formerly unemployed people now get a decent income by creating eye-catching presentations for international business people. I loved going into our office, seeing one of our young workers who just a year ago was unemployed and struggling financially, creating a stellar presentation for a prestigious business. All along the way, our team looked for ways to share the Gospel of Jesus Christ to the people served by this "business as missions" project. I never had to choose between the two in stark, binary fashion.

My favorite classes were the ones we did for homeless teenagers living in the town square. We rented public transportation to get them there and a computer lab at a local university to pull it off. I remember these bedraggled teenagers walking onto campus barefoot, wearing ratty clothes, disheveled in appearance and with intimidated looks on their faces. Many of them were drug addicts, some prostitutes, and all of them seemed ashamed to be at an institution of higher learning. Everything about them cried out, *should we be here?* But they were quick learners and took the lessons seriously. On the last day of the weekly class, I asked them what they wanted to do when they grew up. Without exception, every single one of them said they wanted to become a graphic designer. It may seem silly to teach Adobe Photoshop to people with rotting teeth, inadequate nutrition and who need basic health care and shoes. But I will say they walked out of that class with a little more hope for their futures. And I felt Jesus' joy in it.

Afterward, when we went out to the public square and met with these still homeless teenagers, our team was greeted like heroes. They remembered our names and were touched that we cared about their plight. We shared meals with them, prayers and the Gospel. Our community development project supported our Gospel proclamation and our Gospel proclamation also showed them that we cared about their plight. I won't go as far as some who say we have to "earn the right" to share the Gospel (Jesus' commissions us with His all-encompassing authority, giving us the "ministry of reconciliation" (2 Corinthians 5:18), but I will say it's nice when you have opportunity to do both.

Lifting the Poor

When Jesus said, "The poor you will always have with you," He wasn't sighing and throwing in the towel. His next statement is startling: "And you can help them any time you want" (Mark 14:7). In other words, there are always going to be opportunities to serve the poor. Any time, from the moment you are reading these words until Jesus comes back, we have a white canvas to paint on in the lives of the poor, a blank check on which we can write in any amount. In any one of 24 hours in a day, we can use our creative resources and innovative energy to bless and empower them. When He comes back, I imagine that He will expect us to have availed ourselves of that unlimited opportunity, to spend some of ourselves and our time activating solutions for the complex problems of their lives.

I believe it's easier for people to escape poverty now than at any other time in human history because of the opportunities afforded by globalization. On any spot in the world which has access to the internet you could become a "social entrepreneur" and start an outsourcing business that could lift hundreds of people out of poverty. I've been to a village in Papua, Indonesia that you can't get to by foot. The jungle has repeatedly eaten all attempted roads to get there. The only way in is a five-hour hike through the jungle, a plane ride, or to be born there. Yet they have internet and I marveled at all the kids in that village who were on Facebook! I told a high school principal there, burdened whether his students could ever escape the generational cycles of poverty, that with internet and a few skills these kids could start businesses one day. His marveling surpassed mine.

Jesus has unlimited resources at His disposal to lift the desperate out of their ash heaps. We are those resources! He loves using our creative energies in the lives of others to activate change. There are hundreds of thousands of paintbrushes for this canvas.

It's Complicated

After starting from the base case of gratitude, we've chosen the best kind of motivation (God's heart), we've rejected a false "either/or" dichotomy and now we're proactively weaving ourselves into their stories, expecting to feel God's joy all the way. However to be fair, I need to highlight one messy reality. This is complicated stuff.

I recently attended a disaster relief training put on by a network of churches in our city seeking to help people rebuild their lives in the wake of natural disasters. This area has been hit with forest fires and flooding lately, turning thousands of people's lives upside down. We were being trained on how to shepherd and walk with families through the rebuilding process, and the trainer gave us a warning. "Most of the people that you encounter will really appreciate the help," she said, "but I've got to warn you...some people you meet will try to game the system and try to take advantage of you. You'll find them manipulative and will even lie to you to get more stuff. Just know that going in, it's a mixed bag out there."

Good advice from a practitioner who has purposed in her heart to keep helping needy people, despite the mixed bag of apples that she has encountered.

You'll also not always know the right thing to do, again and again. Those decisions can be stressful and that is demotivating.

I remember sitting inside the dirt-floored shack of man named Pak Sugi, a member of our Indonesian church. On that day I forced my kids to come along for a Sunday afternoon visit to Pak Sugi and his family. Spending more time in slums than malls can help us gain this gift of perspective—something I sincerely desire for my children. For this reason I occasionally forced them to spend time with the poor. Not that they always enjoyed it, but I know it was always good for their hearts.

As we chatted with his family on their thin wicker couch, one of my children suddenly blurted out, "Can we go home now, Daddy?"

I shot a look that meant *not now* to my two kids who were fidgeting and silently begging for a reprieve. To make sure they got my point, I emphasized it in English, as none of the people crowded into this tiny front room would be able understand our native language. "You guys are being rude," I whispered sideways. "Just be patient. They will probably serve us something, we will chat for a while and then we can go home."

I could understand my children's desire to exit that cramped dwelling. It was small, hot, cramped and stuffy. I dragged them there on a Sunday afternoon after a long Indonesian church service, and we had already visited another home in a nearby village. Of course my kids were more excited about the prospect of playing their video game console at home than shallow chit-chatting all afternoon in Indonesian. Their older, slightly ill brother was home doing just that, being watched over by mom. But even though this wasn't something my two younger kids desired at all, I did want them to be comfortable in an impoverished Indonesian world. Besides, I told them afterwards, this is one of the reasons why we moved here.

The assorted family members looked on, standing on the dirt floor and huddled tightly around us. They had to slightly bend over because the roof was so low. Pak Sugi came in carrying a tray filled with five bowls of noodles. "*Tidak usah repot-repot*," I told him, don't go through so much trouble. But he already had and he was very proud to be offering his absolute best to his guests. Rain began to patter outside and kicked up a breeze through the gaping slats of the rickety walls.

We partook of the steaming bowls of noodles and it was pretty good. My son Jordan woofed his down first and Ana picked around at hers. I ate my fill and we chatted some more. It was a little awkward, as there was only enough seating for my two kids, my Indonesian friend and me. The rest of the family remained at hunched-over attention and watched us eat. "Did you build this house yourself?" I asked Sugi after a few more slurpy munches. He said he did and eventually got around to a round-about Javanese hint that he would love some money to build a better roof. "When it rains, there is no place for us to get dry."

The one decoration in the room was a small Santa Claus doll stuck to a nail on the wall. It didn't look to me like the real Santa Claus had ever visited this house. I directed the conversation away from the indirect request for funds. I knew that if he viewed me as his own personal Santa Claus, this would complicate our relationship, though we had helped him before with a medical bill.

We talked some more about his noodle cart business, his new house church group as a new believer, and after a bit I dropped the appropriate cues that it was time for me to get my kids home. On the way home back down the mountain to our comfy house, I complimented the little guys on their mostly good behavior and then I sighed to myself. I feel for this guy, but this is complicated stuff.

Pak Sugi was literally dirt floor poor. I had so much and could have helped him more, and the requests for medical bill help kept on coming after that. His financial assistance requests became so frequent that our team made a policy that we would talk to each other before we helped him. When one of us would say no, he would just bring his garbage collecting pedicab to another team member's house and ask them. We all realized we were creating a dangerous precedent for unhealthy dependency, but I will say it is hard to look in the face of a man who scrapes by on one dollar a day, his family in tow wearing ratty clothes and all the kids with sniffly noses, and say no, so sorry, we can't help you this time.

We did try to "empower" him, giving him that capital for his noodle cart business and loaning him a weed eater so he could make side money as a gardener, but none of those enterprises seemed to make it very far. There were always excuses for why those things didn't take off all the while he kept coming back and asking for more.

It's a wonderfully complex knot—encountering relentless financial need and avoiding unhealthy independence while trying to discern spiritual hunger. Getting involved in their complicated lives means not always knowing the right thing to do.

Even worse and more infuriating is when you try to help the poor and they don't seem to want to help themselves very much. Why do poor people sometimes seem to seal their own doom? Why do people, for instance, who've just received a wad of cash in the form of a micro-finance loan or a one-time government handout, often blow it on something immediate and not invest it into something that could help them in the long run?

A concept that helped me wrestle with this came from a class I took on poverty. In one book we read, *Walking with the Poor*, Brian Myers talked about the "marred identity of the poor."[23] He explains that poverty robs people of their identity as people with inherent worth. From the outside we might judge the poor as just lazy, and although that might be true at times, there are factors that have marred their identity long before we ever meet them.

With the poor we are still dealing with a very basic and low-tech party, the "marred identity" that Meyers writes about. Their broken self-identity tells them they will never escape poverty's clutches, so sometimes they make bad choices in a short term escape from pain.

Even so, the good news is that Jesus is still good news to the poor. He doesn't only want to give them a belly full of bread or just a shoulder to cry on. He wants to totally transform their lives, to un-mar them from the effects of shame, cultural injustices and personal sin. He wants the kingdom of God to invade every corner of their world.

Weaving Into Their Stories

I took my youngest daughter and some of her little friends to Burger King recently, mainly so they could burn off some energy at the play-scape while I worked on my laptop using the free Wi-Fi. After I got all set up, I looked over and noticed a sad looking, older homeless man there. As I was working on this chapter and the theme of reaching out to the poor, I just couldn't in good conscience write on these principles of intentional desperation while intentionally ignoring him (which is what I really felt like doing). So I reluctantly got up, walked over and introduced myself.

His name was Thomas. He had the disheveled look of a homeless man, weathered by the elements in his wrinkled face. He offered for me to take a seat at the booth and as I did, I felt the Lord whisper to me to just be a good listener, nothing more. I asked a few questions and the pain poured out of his sad soul.

He spoke of his divorce from his first wife. He spoke of what it's like to live outdoors. He spoke of his addiction to nicotine and alcohol. But most of all, he spoke of his daughter who was now 47 and whom he hasn't seen since she was two-years-old.

He replayed for me the moment that he got into an awful fight with his wife and just walked out and left them both. It was a terrible, impulsive decision that wrecked his life, to his own admission. Probably theirs, too. I just kept trying to listen and offer the comfort of Christ.

Before I offered to pray for him, I asked, "Thomas, if there was one thing you could ask God for in prayer and get an immediate answer, what would it be?"

He didn't hesitate for a moment. "To see my daughter again."

The pain welled up in his eyes and I went ahead and prayed for him right then.

Not a new house. Not a warm bed. Not a suitcase full of cash. To see his daughter again after 45 years. So much pain in one little lonely man.

Now that you know a little more about Thomas, do you find yourself moved by his story? Is he suddenly not another statistic of homelessness or a question on proper societal response but now a real, live person? Are you rooting for him to turn his life around, maybe even reconcile with his daughter? Me too! That is Jesus' heart in you, which always moves toward restoration and reconciliation.

At first sight, we may see a Thomas on the side of the road begging for money and think, "He's lazy! If I give him money, he'll probably just buy alcohol!" But going a little deeper, thinking about the poor more through heaven's perspective, will help us see them as real live people whom God desperately loves.

While that may be technically true, it's not the whole story, as least not from heaven's side. Keeping a radio talk show host's cold distance from the poor may be the easier choice, but bringing heaven into the equation will ruin us for the ordinary and justifiable response.

Jesus was sent from the Father, full of grace and truth (John 1:14). He came into our world, not only to bring us to truth but also to pour out His abundant grace into our lives. Not one of us deserves even one drop of His mercy, yet He still offers us his grace (which is even more amazing than mercy)! He keeps pouring it out although we keep blowing it. He cares about people, even when they exhibit mixed motives or make dumb choices. He doesn't avoid complicated people. We, too, can be intentional at this, sent from the One who loves them no matter their back stories. Let's choose to weave our stories into the stories of the poor, simply because Jesus does.

Jesus offers the poor and the rich alike the same thing: freedom. Will you join Him in his freedom fight to be good news to the poor?

Father, I confess most of the time I am grumbling about what I don't have rather than all the ways You have abundantly blessed me. I repent of my ungratefulness. My cup overflows and You are its source. Help me to look beyond my own needs and into the lives of the poor with Your creativity and compassion. Thank You that Your Gospel is good news to the poor.

CHAPTER EIGHT

———

THE GRIEVING

Just after the crack of dawn on Sunday, May 27, 2006, a 6.4 earthquake erupted near the city of Jogjakarta in Central Java, Indonesia. It registered at 6.4 on the Richter scale, categorized as level IX, or "maximum intensity destructive." The sudden quake caused 5,700 deaths, 37,000 injuries and financial losses of 3.6 billion U.S. dollars.

Those are the cold hard facts, but I want to introduce you to some of the people. Pak Suri was one of those 37,000 injured and his wife and son were two of the 5,700 deaths. He was a rice farmer, living near the large city of Jogjakarta in an outlying town called Bantul. Like most Indonesians, and especially farmers, he was already up by 4 a.m. and preparing to work the small field near his simple home. His wife and son were also out gathering tools from their shed in preparation for the day's routine work.

Pak Suri remembered he needed something back at the house for the day's work and went back to retrieve it. His house was a simple structure, built with his own hands along with help from his neighbors. Brick walls with large cracks running through the mortar. Bare cement floors. Ceramic tiles on the tilting roof. Not bad for a farmer in Bantul—in fact Suri's family would probably be considered middle class there—but his home was nowhere near the specs to be able to withstand even a moderate earthquake.

He remembers finding the tool from under his bed when the shaking started. He turned in shock and by the time he made it to the doorway, just a few short feet away, the tiles from the roof starting falling on his head and cracking on the floor all around him. He screamed for his wife and his son who were outside near the shed where they kept their other farming tools. The beams were falling from that even more rickety structure and striking them on the head as they tried in vain to protect themselves. They were dead by the time he could climb through the rubble and get to them.

As he held them both and looked around at his leveled house, he began sobbing in deep heaves. He had lost everything that was most precious to him—his wife whom he had been married to for over 22 years and his 9-year-old son. Although he knew he should feel grateful to Allah for being allowed to live, deep down he had wanted to die right there with his wife and son.

My son and I met Pak Suri as our Indonesian church was trying to help people displaced by the disaster. Bantul looked to me as if a nuclear bomb had gone off and Suri was one of the many people we met picking through the literal rubble of their lives.

I remember him pointing to the spot near the shed where he lost his wife and son. He told us his awful story, mixing in his theology that Allah had willed this to happen to him, probably to test his faith. He really shouldn't complain, he told us.

His was one of the last houses of the day our small team was serving. I asked him if we could get him anything.

"A pillow would be nice," he said after a few moments.

A pillow? Behind him his home was completely leveled into a chaotic pile of bricks, he had no electricity, running water or easy access to food. His surviving teenage son was picking through the wreckage of their ruined lives. Of course he needed more than a pillow, but that was the first thing that popped into his shell-shocked head, probably still sore from sleeping on a concrete slab the night before.

I tried to give him more than a pillow. I told my own son to come a little closer and we stood with him. I put my arm around Pak Suri. I told him how sorry I was that all these unfathomable things had happened to him. I prayed for him and tried to offer comfort.

Later we did bring him a real pillow and felt a little silly doing so. I remember walking up to his devastated house, our team waiting in the van in the road, and handing a man who had lost everything a nylon bag of synthetic fibers. But he smiled and genuinely appreciated it. I think he was more touched that someone was touched by his story, and the pillow was just a little extra reminder of that.

Comfort Medics

I believe natural disasters should be the church's finest hour. We as believers have access to the comfort of God in our lives and we can be dispatched to pockets of great pain and suffering all over the earth where shell-shocked victims and survivors await that urgently needed commodity—comfort for the grieving.

Each of our fellowships can dispatch a mobile medic unit of comfort into any zone where the wounded are recovering. I've had the sober privilege of serving on a few of these comfort brigades, traveling to places reeling from various natural disasters.

After Hurricane Katrina, a small team from our church in Austin, Texas, went door-to-door in a Mississippi Gulf Coast town wrecked by the fury of that unprecedented disaster. We felt so limited with a van full of hastily bought supplies and a team of only three. But we did have an ample supply of Christ's comfort.

I remember while we were working through one neighborhood, we saw a lady sitting on the stoop of her beach house with her head down, with her husband sitting listless beside her. Behind them was their completely collapsed house.

"Need any water?" we called out from our van passing by.

"No, we've got some, thanks," she called back.

We stopped anyway and chatted with them, hearing their familiar story of devastation. Her heart was broken because she hadn't been able to find her family photos all strewn out in the wreckage. She opened up to us, sharing her uncertainty about where they would live now. Her daughter, a freshman in college, had invited them to come and live with her in her college apartment. But taking her daughter up on that generous offer burdened her greatly. "I don't want to ruin her college experience!" she lamented. Yet she could think of no other good options. All the complications of her life that this storm had wrought came tumbling out of her.

We listened. We put our arms around them and requested permission to pray. As we asked God to come into their hopeless and complex situation, I felt her heavy-set body start heaving up and down with deep cries. Her husband opened up too and we prayed for him. The two of them had a good cry right on the front porch of their former home, in front of three total strangers.

They felt comforted. Their tears needed release.

These afflicted ones do have urgent needs and we need to be proactive at lifting them out of the pressing problems that weigh down upon them. But way down below their very real and urgent needs, their souls are craving the comfort of Christ. As image bearers of God we have an abundance to deliver to them.

The Master Comforter

How did our master, the Wonderful Counselor, the perfect picture of the heart of God, comfort people?

> When Mary reached the place where Jesus was and saw Him, she fell at His feet and said, "Lord, if You had been here, my brother would not have died."
>
> When Jesus saw her weeping, and the Jews who had come along with her also weeping, He was deeply moved in spirit and troubled. "Where have you laid him?" He asked.
>
> "Come and see, Lord," they replied.
>
> Jesus wept.

Then the Jews said, "See how He loved him!" (John 11:32-36)

He wept—probably one of the most famous verses in the Bible. It's at least the most popular for a group of sixth graders in Sunday School challenged to cite a verse they have previously memorized. Short and to the point.

On that devastating day, Jesus had a good cry with Martha and Mary. He didn't say, "Now, wait a minute. I'm the master of the universe here, and in just a few moments I'm going to resurrect your dead brother. Where is your faith?" Instead, their hurting hearts touched His heart deeply enough to evoke tears out of the creator of the universe. It seems His response to fear was often an assertion of His authority but His response to pain was unabashed empathy. Although He always sees the light at the end of the tunnel, He sympathizes with those of us still groping along inside the darkness.

Jesus is the "image of the invisible God" (Colossians 1:15), the One who splashed waterfalls into existence with the tip of His finger. He shaped the towering ice pinnacles of the Himalayan Mountains with the breath of His words. The One who saw into the lifeless, murky void and with burning stars forged the sparkly Milky Way. "For by Him all things were created...all things have been created through Him and for Him" (Colossians 1:15-16). Yet on that afternoon, this perfect mint image of God invited us in to see how human tragedy breaks His heart. He is not the unmoved mover. That simply isn't the picture that emerges when you read the stories of the heart of God beating inside the body of Jesus. He doesn't observe our grief from a safe distance, solely concerned only with shaping our characters. Our Creator sat right down with Martha and Mary and had a good cry.

Notice how the Jewish onlookers responded. The thought "See how perfect His theology is," did not escape their gaped-open mouths. Instead they marveled, "See how He loved him" (John 11:36).

The tears in this story reveal how much God loves you and how broken He is over the injustice and abuse that has befallen you. He not only took your sins upon Himself, as prophesied in Isaiah 53, but this suffering servant also carries your deepest sorrows (Isaiah 53:4).

He carries our sorrows and He carries theirs. Yet what is our first reaction, as smiley-faced, Christian-countenanced people to other people who are in pain? We want to cheer them up. We want to make them feel better. It's going to be all right. There is light at the end of the tunnel. Plenty more fish in the sea. You'll look back on this one day and be thankful that this experience strengthened your character. That happened to me once and here's how I overcame, etc. etc.

But when you are in pain, what does your own heart crave? Probably the last thing it wants is a pep-talk from a well-meaning believer.

My Father's Eyes

When I was nine-years-old, my beloved black Labrador puppy, Poco, was run over by a car right in front of our house. I ran to my room, dove into my bed and cried my little eyes out. When my father came home and found out what happened, he came into my room and knelt by my bed with me. Through my heaves and sniffles I looked up and saw something that shocked me: tears in my father's eyes. Real tears! He knelt beside the bed and held my limp hand and tried to hide his own tears from me. My big strong dad was crying over my heartbreak.

But I'm so grateful I saw them. I'm so glad he didn't say, as some of us might imagine God saying, something like "That will teach you to leave the gate open." A God unmoved by my pain, coldly detached and recording my reaction on a character improvement checklist, is not the kind of God I can fall in love with, share my secrets with and follow wholeheartedly.

To comfort well, you may need to look up from your place of pain just long enough to see the tears in the eyes of your big, strong Father. You affect Him.

They affect Him.

Too Far for Comfort

The church is a lot of things. A friend of mine starting churches in modern-day Macedonia says that a healthy community of faith has five functions, all of them held in dynamic tension with each other:

The church is a temple. We minister unto God and on behalf of people.

The church is a family. We enjoy fellowship with one another and feel loved and accepted.

The church is an army. We advance the kingdom reign of God into dark places.

The church is a school. We receive instruction and disciple others in the ways of God.

The church is a hospital. We give and receive the comfort of God.

I love the local church dearly. I love seeing a community of believers before God in sweet worship, gathering together in living rooms for Bible studies, meeting together in small clusters for mentoring, stretching outward on short-term mission trips, caring for the poor and sometimes just goofing off, enjoying life and inside jokes together.

Healthy churches are infused with the dynamic tension of all these seemingly competing roles right next to each other in one community. But the last one—the church is a hospital—I long to see that have more of a place in our communities of faith. The church should be the safest place on earth to find healing and recovery. But usually it's the one place people feel the most pressure to fake it and paint a brave face over their internal misery.

How do you feel at your small group when you open up to some place of pain in your life, and someone pulls out their machine gun of encouragement and mows you down with good advice? You smile, thank them for their kind words, grab a throw pillow from their sofa and clutch it tightly on your lap. Then you make a mental note to yourself to never, ever, be vulnerable here again.

What's wrong with this very common picture? God knows we need good advice sometimes. We do need encouragement. But what we generally need first is comfort, which at its core Greek essence means "a calling to one's side." We need someone to simply walk beside us in those moments, because our hearts need comfort before our minds can receive truth. To our hurting friends we usually first pull out a truth that is aimed at their minds. We give them Romans 8:28: "In all things God works for the good of those who love Hm, who have been called according to His purpose," but what their hearts really need in that moment is Romans 12:15: "Rejoice with those who rejoice; mourn with those who mourn."

I was first impacted with these concepts through the teachings of Intimate Life Ministries. The director of that counseling and teaching ministry, David Ferguson, writes, "The ministry of comfort is not about trying to 'fix' people, correct them, or motivate them with a pep talk. Such efforts may help at times, but they do not bring comfort. The God of comfort gives hope and strength and eases pain in a hurting person when we compassionately mourn that hurt with them."[24]

He goes on to explain this well-known but under-used verse on comfort:

> Blessed be the God and Father of our Lord Jesus Christ, the Father of mercies and God of all comfort, who comforts us in all our affliction so that we will be able to comfort those who are in any affliction with the comfort with which we ourselves are comforted by God. (2 Corinthians 1:3, NASB)

The God of comfort wants to reveal His comfort through us. "It's not that God's comfort is insufficient or ineffective," Ferguson continues, "but He has chosen to share the ministry of meeting relational needs with us as we love our neighbors. If we fail, for example, to 'comfort those in any trouble with the comfort we ourselves have received' (2 Corinthians 1:4), people suffer a degree of relational aloneness that we are designed and called to fill. When this happens, our ministry of the truth to them is, at least in part, irrelevant."[25] Ouch.

Seeing Past the Bad

Another reason we miss hurting hearts in this is because we focus on the bad behaviors of people in pain. Sometimes, like us, they do things that deserve correction. And that's all we see.

But there is usually more to the story, a backstory. I know a counselor named Kyle Miller who uses a framework he calls the Sad>Mad>Bad cycle.[26] First there is sadness, followed by anger, then the acting out in sin.

The only way to break this cycle, Kyle says, is to help people bring their initial Sad to Jesus. There they can mourn out their Sad by forgiving others and repenting of their own sin, experiencing God's deep comfort in the here and now. Over time, Jesus' comfort shrinks the Sad and the knee-jerk Mad and exploding Bad so that we can grow in His grace and truth with others in relationship.

"Blessed are those who mourn," Jesus told a crowd experiencing the ups and downs and life, "for they shall be comforted" (Matthew 5:4). God has a heart for people in pain, and we can always start there.

Advancing Comfort

There are survivors in your town, maybe not just from a natural disaster, but those "who are in any affliction" walking around dazed and overwhelmed at the complexity, relentlessness and weight of their problems. You can spot them easily as the people with the weight of the world on their hunched-over shoulders. Their situation is way beyond needing some good advice just yet. They need the comfort of God this very moment.

The single mom still angry over the betrayal and overwhelmed with the prospect of raising two children by herself. The sullen teenager who keeps cutting her arms and legs for reasons she can't fully understand. The successful businessman driving home on his commute who can't think of one good reason to go on living. The couple who stumbles out of the doctor's office dazed with the diagnosis that the baby they are expecting has been stricken with Down's syndrome. The sex addict who strayed past the bounds of normalcy for a more exciting sexual experience, now hit with the news that he is HIV positive. The young family who can think of no other financial options than bankruptcy. The aging wife who is taking care of a husband who no longer recognizes her.

We're not going to run out of work anytime soon if our job is to bring the comfort of God to a people in pain. Let's look past the broken things they do and into their broken hearts.

First, receive the comfort of God for your own broken heart. Then give that same comfort out generously to the broken around you, the people who have been drop kicked by cruel circumstances and ruined by their own choices. You won't have to look very far to find the ones who need to see tears in their Father's eyes.

God of all comfort, please comfort my broken heart. Thank You for giving me the permission to grieve. I'm grateful that You cry with me over my heartaches and that You carry my sorrows. I open my soul to You. Please soothe those dry places in me where I have become crusty and unmoved by the plight of others. I know my heart needs to be softened with Your tears. Weep through me. Listen through me. Use me to bring Your deep comfort to the broken and desperate in my city.

CHAPTER NINE

———

THE LOST

It was the last show of the day and it finished right at park closing time. My wife, two kids, in-laws and I had just enjoyed a theatrical production of *The Lion King* at Disney World's newly opened park, Animal Kingdom. We strapped our baby girl in her stroller, gathered up all our bags and trinkets and took a deep breath for the exiting process.

As we made our way toward the exits, a concession worker from a corn dog stand came out and offered people passing by free corn dogs. Wait, what…I love corn dogs! My father-in-law and I scooped up as many as we could for a convenient dinner as throngs of people streamed past us toward the parking lots.

One for you. Here you go. One for you. One for you. Hey, where's Caleb? Caleb? Caleb? Has anyone seen Caleb?

Nana looked up one street, Pop looked down the other, mom checked the immediate area as I dashed back into the theater, thinking maybe our four-year-old little adventurer had wandered back in. No Caleb.

We gathered back together to make a search plan, pushing the worst fears out of our minds. All of us split up in different directions and starting calling out his name in earnest. *Caleb!*

I quickly threaded my way through the dense crowd, imagining my little boy crying and lost somewhere in that sea of park goers. As the seconds dragged on to minutes, I tried to push out of my mind horrible words like *kidnapped* or *predator* and kept on searching. *Caleb!*

I began yelling out his name and jumping up on park benches to better scan the crowd. At no point did I consider my reputation or what these hundreds of people might be thinking of a frantic, shouting man. I looked like a fool but didn't care. I was desperate to find my son.

After a few more dreadful minutes of searching, suddenly his familiar, cute little blonde head poked out from behind a kiosk of souvenirs. A worker was holding his little hand, searching the crowd for this lost little boy's parents. I heartily thanked the man and lifted up Caleb into an explosion of a bear hug, kissing his cheeks while trying to hold back my own tears.

I was so relieved to see my little buddy again I didn't even think of scolding him, like, *Caleb, don't ever leave us like that. Always hold mommy's hand and make sure you are always with us.* Nothing like that. He actually had remembered that if he ever got lost, find someone with a name tag, which he did. I just held him tightly and quickly carried him back to our anxious family. The only thing that mattered was having my precious son in my arms again. Celebratory relief welcomed us at the reunion.

There was a father once, an even more desperate one, who also looked like a fool but didn't care. In his culture fathers were revered, respected and feared. They were almost like kings, authority figures on thrones willing to receive an audience but never going out in search of one.

But this father was different. He was so broken by the hard-hearted betrayal of his youngest son that his grueling days were filled with despair. On one hot afternoon he saw a figure approaching on the dusty road leading to his farmhouse...*it couldn't be*. He jumped up from the porch and strained his eyes to get a better look...*it sure looks like him*. He called to his servants and they affirmed their master's improbable hope...*your son has come back home*. The father tore off his porch like lightning and did something that soon became the scandalous gossip of his community. He actually lifted the bottom of his robe so he could run faster, baring his legs before his shocked servants, and ran toward his scoundrel of a son. Think of it! This respected pillar of the community going off to greet the very wretch who broke his heart and wasted his hard-earned money. Not only that, but the old fool welcomed the bankrupt loser as if he were a returning champion:

> But the father said to his servants, "Quick! Bring the best robe and put it on him. Put a ring on his finger and sandals on his feet. Bring the fattened calf and kill it. Let's have a feast and celebrate. For this son of mine was dead and is alive again; he was lost and is found." (Luke 15:22-24)

This father was so lovesick for this lost son he didn't care about his reputation. He couldn't even bring himself to scold his son for his sinful squandering. Joy couldn't be held back over being reunited with someone more valuable than all his possessions combined.

His oldest son didn't appreciate all the merry-making over his decrepit brother and refused to come into the house from the field at the request of his dad. He was so incensed that he actually spurned a direct command from his own father!

> The older brother became angry and refused to go in. So his father went out and pleaded with him. (Luke 15:28)

Once again this father had to set aside his reputation, already in tatters, to go and seek out his other son. It should be them coming to him and here he is seeking out another son who should know better—how disgraceful! A few verses later we find the reason behind the father's incomprehensible behavior:

> "My son," the father said, "you are always with me, and everything I have is yours. But we had to celebrate and be glad, because this brother of yours was dead and is alive again; he was lost and is found." (Luke 15:31-32)

He was lost and is found. That was reason enough for the God of heaven to set aside his dignity and go off in search for you. God is a lovesick father, the desperate dad who has no greater joy than getting His lost children back and embracing them tightly. That's how valuable you are to Him.

Let the Father's love embrace you today, washing away all your shame. Jesus hanging naked on a despicable cross is proof enough of how far He would be willing to set aside His dignity to get you back. You might feel like turning away when He hugs you, or squirming when He puts the best robe on you, a ring on your finger and new sandals on your feet. You know more than anyone how unworthy you are. But just try anyway to rest in the assurance of His dauntless love as you feast together.

As you are filled up with the Father's intense and personal love for you, don't keep it to yourself. Let it surge up to the brim of your soul and begin splashing out into the cold darkness around you. Become as desperate to seek and save as He is. Let His heartbeat for the lost become the rhythm of your life.

Compelled to Implore

"The Son of Man came to seek and save what was lost" (Luke 19:10). Jesus likened Himself to a good shepherd who leaves the ninety-nine sheep safely tucked away in the sheep pen, endures the elements of the open country and searches high and low for the one sheep that has strayed away.

> And when he finds it, he joyfully puts it on his shoulders and goes home. Then he calls his friends and neighbors together and says, "Rejoice with me; I have found my lost sheep." (Luke 15:5-6)

Rejoice with me. You can't help but feel God's joy in His mission to restore broken relationships, bodies, minds, hearts and souls. You'll even be refreshed in the revelation of His own love toward you. This is the reason Paul wrote to his good buddy Philemon, "I pray that you may be active in sharing your faith, so that you will have a full understanding of every good thing we have in Christ" (Philemon 1:6).

The way to have a full understanding of every good thing we have in Christ is to be intentional about sharing your faith. *Wow, God, You really do love people. I can feel it when I share You with others. Do You really feel like that about me?* Try it and see.

> For Christ's love *compels* us, because we are convinced that one died for all, and therefore all died...We are therefore Christ's ambassadors, as though God were making His appeal through us. We *implore* you on Christ's behalf: Be reconciled to God. (2 Corinthians 5:14 & 20)

Christ's love is not something that can be cooped up within your own soul, for your own personal salvation only, but it compels itself outward. Evangelism was never designed to be a religious chore that you are supposed to do, a duty about as much fun as flossing your teeth. Feeling guilty about not witnessing is yesterday's smallness. The love of Christ, the compassion in His eyes for the lost, will give you the want-to and launch you into a life of imploring.

Yesterday, I went out to a local mall to share good news with people. Going in, I felt a bit down emotionally and didn't really feel like doing it. But I had already made a plan to meet some other people in the food court to go out and share, so I followed through. After meeting my friends in the food court and praying together, we went out and had several good spiritual conversations. There were a lot of internationals working at the little kiosks in the middle of the mall, sitting there bored and playing on their smartphones. It was easy to strike up conversations. I got to share the above story of the prodigal son with a former Israeli soldier who was working at one of those kiosks. He was surprised at the ending and smiled at the Father's response. We all came away from that outreach outing with a smile on our faces, too. It reawakened in us the goodness of the good news.

Leaning Into Adventure

A hero of mine who lives out this value is my former pastor and spiritual mentor, Ron Parrish. When he was turning 50, Ron decided to forego the typical mid-life crisis and go on a great adventure. He had heard about other men trying to get in touch with their inner wild man by going on risky adventure trips. But he had something a little different in mind. I remember him asking aloud, "I guess I could go bear hunting in Alaska or maybe some serious mountain climbing somewhere. But why not focus on bringing the Gospel to some unreached people group?"

For him the greatest adventure would have to be linked to Christ's mission to seek and save the lost. He started scheming. Why not take his three weeks of vacation and find a pocket of darkness somewhere on the earth where Jesus had not been named, put on his shoes of readiness to share the Gospel of peace and just see what would happen?

He had served as a missionary to Indonesia for years so it was easy for him to make his adventure plans on the archipelago. He had a lot of contacts there and was familiar with lots of unreached people groups on various islands. He was also fluent in the language which didn't hurt. After prayer and planning he settled on an island named Sumbawa, just two islands east of the famous resort island of Bali. This small island, a much more remote and poorer island than Bali, is home to 600,000 Muslims and they are known for being hard-core in their religion. There were some risks (like getting caught and being imprisoned), but Ron calculated the potential reward (winning a key person to Christ who could launch a kingdom movement on the island) would be well worth it.

Ron started makings plans for his trip, and he informed the missionaries from our church serving in Indonesia at the time that he was coming over, not so much on a pastoral visit but more for an evangelistic road trip.

We were intrigued with his idea and Ron invited along the three of us men serving in Indonesia at the time. The sweetener in the deal for us was Ron's plan to traverse the island by motorcycle. How cool to be riding around a tropical island every day on a motorcycle, the breeze in our hair, just going wherever the wind would take us. He describes one event in his potent little book, *From Duty to Delight*: *Finding Greater Joy in Daily Prayer*:

> I was on a mission trip on a remote island in Indonesia. We had shared Christ with dozens of Muslims. Our prayer was for a key individual (the man of peace—see Luke 10) who would respond to the Gospel and in turn influence his (or her) friends...Several people had prayed to receive Christ, but none of them had seemed to be the key individual that could be part of a church planting movement. We were to leave that part of the island and head back to Bali in two days. I was watching the sun come up at a dock where fishing boats unload their night's catch. I prayed "Lord,

it's not happening. I'm about to leave this place and I feel so fruitless. I feel like I've been fishing all night and haven't caught any fish. What's up with this?" I was in lamenting mode.

I turned around and there was a man standing behind me named Agus who had come to watch the sunrise. Agus turned out to be very interested in the Gospel. So interested, he wanted to hear more. So we set an appointment to meet again later that morning. He didn't turn to Christ (while we were there) but he introduced me to Ibrahim, Yusuf, Aman, and Elias—all who listened intently to the Good News and prayed to receive Christ! Elias turned out to be a very influential man among the shrimp farmers of the area. We believe he is the man of peace for whom we had been praying. Like the disciples of old, Jesus told me where to cast my net. God meets us in our disappointment, even when things don't turn out as we had hoped.[27]

Ron still talks about that trip with a gleam of joy in his eyes. Beyond just leaning into adventure for adventure's sake, he continues to dream kingdom dreams and feels deeply disappointed when they don't come true. And what inspires me the most is that year after year Ron keeps working hard and crying out to God for those breakthroughs. His heart is fully alive because it is infused with the hope of heaven.

When I first started to follow Christ at age 16, I couldn't shake this slight fear that God was going to make me weird. I remember asking an older guy in our youth group, "If we become fanatics, would we know it?" He said he wasn't sure. I was imagining myself, without even realizing it, becoming a cranky person with religious bad breath who berates people who seem to be having a good time.

That kind of thinking was reinforced when I would hear people say something like, "Never tell God you won't do something, because that's the very thing He'll make you do!" That paradigm frames God as an eternal killjoy who delights in making you miserable. If I were really spiritual, or so I thought, God would make my life extremely horrible, maybe forcing me to marry a cranky, unsightly woman and become a missionary to some Godforsaken country.

For the record, I'm happy to say I married a cheerful, beautiful woman and became a missionary to Indonesia (beautiful also, and not Godforsaken in the slightest). Instead of being doomed to a life of corn mush and monk-like austerity, surrendering to Jesus has filled my life with a joy that at times "knows no bounds" as Paul put it (2 Corinthians 7:4). There's no greater joy I know of than having front row seats to see God's redeeming hand in people's broken lives.

Interception

I've got a good friend whom I'll call Colby who came to visit us in Texas recently. He also stayed with our family when we lived in Indonesia, helping out at our empowerment center and was my motorcycle traveling companion for a few mini-adventures. I've appreciated all the generous ways he has financially supported our ministry in Indonesia over the years, but more than that I just enjoy his friendship and company.

I can remember when Colby's life was much more hopeless.

As an incoming freshman at the University of Texas at Austin, Colby was determined to escape the alcoholism, drug use and depression that had plagued him during his high school years. Despite his good intentions, he quickly fell back into the partying crowd. He got a little carried away one night and was thrown into the city slammer for public drunkenness. Sitting in a cold jail cell, still wearing a shirt caked with his own vomit, he felt like giving up on life. It surprised him how ambivalent he felt about continuing to live there at rock bottom.

He was released the next morning and made it back to campus. Later that week he noticed a group of students in front of his dorm giving out free snow cones. A banner tacked on to their table declared, "Hope Student Fellowship." His eyes fixated on the word *hope*. He thought they were the Peace Corps or something and felt compelled to come over. The feeling was so strong he tried to fight it and later said he felt like a magnet was pulling him toward that snow cone table.

Earlier in the morning the group of students zealous for Jesus had prayed, "Lord, intercept someone's life on this very spot today." They saw Colby approaching, gave him a snow cone and started some friendly chit-chat about his brand new college career. They also invited him to attend a picnic they were having later. He showed up tentatively and although he felt very guarded, he enjoyed meeting some friendly people and scoring a free meal. He started coming to weekly worship meetings and felt his heart warming toward God. Yet he also felt the pull toward hard partying with new friends on his dormitory hall.

After three weeks of living in both worlds, he showed up at a Friday night worship meeting and watched the other students worship Jesus with joyful abandon, while his own pockets were filled with the drugs that continued to enslave him. He said later about that evening, "I was ashamed. I was incredibly aware that it was wrong. I felt like the stuff in my pockets would radiate some kind of signal that would announce to other people my guilt."

The next day was the group's fall retreat and Colby said he planned to attend. But in the fog of his hangover the next morning, he didn't hear the phone calls from his new friends who were going to pick up him and bring him to the retreat. Their repeated phone calls and bangs on his dorm room door in the morning could not summon him from his slumber and they were forced to go on without him to the retreat, which was about two hours from campus.

They arrived at the retreat without Colby. We had been praying for Colby and sensed he was really close to the kingdom, yet could still see him bound by the enticements of the world. I was very disappointed that he didn't come, but I made another call to his dorm room for one more try. He answered groggily.

"Uh...hello?"

"Hey Colby, it's Mike. What happened, man?"

"Oh, the retreat. Dude, I totally forgot."

I then remembered one student who was coming to the retreat later and asked if he would be willing to come with her. He agreed, she drove him and that night Colby prayed to receive Christ into his life. It was such an amazing moment. I remember looking at one of the student leaders named Clark who had been praying for Colby fervently over the course of the semester. From his dorm room window Clark would see Colby smoking with his friends down at the courtyard and would zap him with repeated prayers. Clark and I silently smiled at each other, marveling at a living, breathing answer to prayer.

Colby got off the drugs and took off like a rocket spiritually. He became filled with the same joy that he had envied in the other students he first encountered. He led a small group in his hall and brought to Christ three students who lived there under Colby's evangelistic gun sights.

That all happened when Colby was 18 and now as a man in his forties he is still following Jesus. Life has given him a few hard knocks but he has remained steady. The guys whom he led to Christ are also still going strong. One of them, an uninterested atheist when Colby first met him on his dorm room floor, became the college pastor for the same campus group, which is still intercepting people as hopeless as Colby and bringing them into the kingdom.

Now consider the story from heaven's perspective. God the Father had been loving Colby for millennia, even before he was born, "with an everlasting love" (Jeremiah 31:3). As a boy, Colby caught glimpses of God's Word through infrequent church visits, but it never took root and the Father was disappointed. For years He whispered to Colby's guilty conscience about his need for forgiveness but to no avail. How the Father's heart broke when his Colby was snared in drug addiction and hit rock bottom at such a young age. Finally the moment came when the Father orchestrated Colby to walk out in front of his dorm and meet a group of friendly students offering snow cones.

Colby's heart thawed in an atmosphere of lavish worship to Jesus and his spirit was stirred hearing stories of this same Jesus. All of heaven held its breath as beloved Colby lifted up his first clumsy prayers of sincerity. After a few false starts, Colby finally came to his senses and recognized his need for mercy. Heaven rejoiced with gusto when Colby finally walked down that road of humility and reconciled with the Father.

I'm hooked on ministry to the desperate. What could be more exhilarating than watching desperate people like Colby getting pulled out of the mud and mire by God's mighty hand? And then after that seeing more kingdom stories unfold? Bungee jumping maybe? I've never done it but I don't think so. I can't believe there's any greater fun, home or abroad, than to play supporting roles in these unfolding seek and save dramas, to be Jesus' sidekick when He shows up in the places where the enemy is strong.

I just can't get enough.

A Tale of Two Trash Pickers

Bram and Desto worked as trash pickers and lived in a shantytown on the outskirts of Malang, Indonesia. Every morning and afternoon, just like the other 100 or so able-bodied men and woman of their slum, they combed through trash containers in front of people's houses looking for things that can be sold or recycled back to local factories.

There is a system in their community. The slum lord charges them about $3 US a month to live in one of the dirt-floored and dusty cement shacks. From what the trash pickers find on their daily rounds, they sell, barter or share amongst themselves and give a portion back to the slum lord. Each shack is both a home and a storage unit. One room of the dwelling is for sleeping and cooking and living, and the other is for storing the items they seek, mostly cardboard and water bottles. There is no running water and people make use of the polluted river that flows nearby. An intermittent flow of electricity dimly lights the bare bulbs in their homes. There are no permits for these shelters, built mostly with discarded plywood, bamboo and advertising banners that were found in the streets. Even with all that is lacking, there is an ample supply of friendliness and hospitality to visitors.

One humid Thursday afternoon, my American teammate John and I walked through their dusty streets at the suggestion of a friend who wanted to start an outreach there. There we were, just two out-of-place foreigners walking through this poor community, nodding and smiling at people, praying under our breath and asking the Lord to lead us to hungry hearts. Bram and Desto came out of their little shacks and were very interested to meet and greet two visitors from afar.

Before we got to the Good News, we got to know them. Bram grew up on the island of Kalimantan (formerly Borneo). He had dreams of a good life, starting a family and maybe becoming successful. Now he was living under the very bottom rung of the rickety socio-economic ladder of Indonesia. Desto had a similar poverty-stricken backstory. Both said they were Muslim. When Desto told us he attended a Catholic school as a boy, we steered the conversation toward Jesus.

Once we waded into these waters, Desto immediately got into debate mode. He started ticking off a common list of objections against Christianity, but Bram seemed more tender and open. When we talked about God's solution for the problem of sin, Bram mused aloud, "Maybe Allah is punishing me for all the sins of my life. I keep praying that He will show me a new way, but you can see for yourselves how I am living."

The next week we came back with an Indonesian teammate for a second visit and learned that Desto was still out on his daily rounds. However Bram was there and he invited us in. We sat cross-legged on the simple rug of his sleeping quarter, barely enough room for the four of us. He kept going back to the theme of his own failings and the justice of Allah. Then he pulled out the *Injil* (New Testament) that we had given him the previous week. "You know, I have been reading this a little. I like the story of the lady who was bleeding for twelve years and she grabbed the edge of Jesus' cloak, and she was instantly healed. That was amazing."

"Wow, Bram, we're so glad you've been reading these stories in the *Injil*! You will find that Jesus is a friend to people who feel hopeless, just like that lady who couldn't stop bleeding." The three of us stole glad glances at each other.

"Well, I like these stories. I just haven't gotten very far yet."

"How far?"

"I read all of Matthew and I'm halfway through Mark now."

That's way more than I read in one week, I thought to myself. I loved his hunger and felt my faith stirring that he could be the "man of peace" in the community, the one responsive soul that could launch a movement in this place.

He shared more of his heart with us, we prayed for his burdens and our Indonesian partner offered to start a Bible study in his home on Friday evenings. Bram readily accepted and said he would invite a friend.

"These stories haven't really impacted my heart yet," he said, "but they are so interesting. I want to keep reading."

Sounds like a promising start to a story? Our Indonesian partner kept going out there, they continued to study together but over time Bram seemed to lose interest. At the same time, Desto the Debater became more and more open. He asked our

Indonesian friend for prayers for deliverance against some demonic torment in his life. Jesus delivered him immediately.

He went home and prayed for his daughter in Jesus' Name and she was also immediately delivered from her demonic oppression. After that he was sold and became very zealous for his new Savior. He invited others in his community to investigate the claims of Christ in the *Injil*. He prayed for the sick and some of them were healed. He challenged people who chose to follow Jesus to be baptized publicly, not an easy thing to do in a community that threatened expulsion for such a traitorous act.

Since then there have been stories of salvation, baptisms, deliverance, healings and persecution, all under Desto's leadership. Just recently I received this email report from the friend who first suggested that we prayerwalk this shantytown:

> Two weeks ago "Sita" was kicked out of her house because of becoming a follower of Jesus. She was beaten and her belongings were thrown out into the street at about 4 a.m. in the morning. Her son-in-law took her Bible, burned it publicly, then proceeded to urinate on it. A number of people (including other followers of Jesus) in the community watched as all of this took place. Not long after this incident, the wife of the man who set the Bible on fire (Sita's daughter) got sick. These new believers decided to take up a collection amongst themselves (remember these are very poor people) and give it to their persecutor so he could get some help for his wife. After seeing this act of love and grace, a family who had also

witnessed the Bible-burning incident has now become interested in learning from the Bible and about how to follow Jesus! Please pray for the believers in this community of trash collectors as they experience persecution. Pray that they would be filled with strength and grace to remain strong and true to Jesus.[28]

The kingdom of heaven is breaking out in this community. Who knows how far those ripples will keep going, as Desto's disciples lead others to Christ, echoing down the family tree branches of eternity. It's amazing to me that it all started with a friend and I doing a simple 45-minute prayerwalk one afternoon, carrying with us no grand strategies. We just spread out a handful of simple Gospel seeds into the soil of hungry hearts.

Jesus talked about the potency of those seeds we carry in our pockets, painting the kingdom of God like this:

> It is like a mustard seed, which is the smallest seed you plant in the ground. Yet when planted, it grows and becomes the largest of all garden plants, with such big branches that the birds of the air can perch in its shade. (Mark 4:31-32)

You never know what is going to happen to those seeds. Sometimes they are immediately rejected. Sometimes they shoot up quickly, as in Bram's case, but wither under the sun's cruel heat. Sometimes the thorns representing "life's worries, riches and pleasures" choke them out (Luke 8:14). In Jesus' parable of the sower, He seems to say that three out of four times the seeds are not going to make it to full-grown maturity.

But when you do find that fourth kind of soil, the rich soil, those open hearts who hear the Word, retain it and let loose a movement of multiplying kingdom life...whoa and wow! What a joy to hit pay dirt! We can almost hear the celebration of heaven, resonating from the Father's heart, when one of His lost ones is finally found and grounded. "In the same way, I tell you, there is rejoicing in the presence of the angels of God over one sinner who repents" (Luke 15:10).

Jesus is the author of these amazing stories. It was His heart to intercept Colby from a life of hopelessness and drug addiction and to restore him into a life of meaning and purpose. It was His idea to transform Desto the trash collector into Desto the house church network leader. He is always seeking and saving the lost and thinking up more story lines than we could ever pursue. He's got His eye on some folks in your community. There are stories to be told from the deadened lives of your friends, neighbors, co-workers, relatives and even strangers, and He's already got the ending in mind. The storyline goes something like this:

> He lifted me out of the slimy pit,
> out of the mud and mire;
> He set my feet on a rock
> and gave me a firm place to stand.
> He put a new song in my mouth,
> a hymn of praise to our God.
> Many will see and fear
> and put their trust in the Lord. (Psalm 40:2-3)

What an amazing privilege to play supporting roles in these redemptive dramas! Maybe your part is simply at the beginning, when the seed is first planted. Or maybe it comes later, like when my Indonesian friend spent many, many hours in Desto's community mentoring this new believer toward maturity. Paul summed up the success of a church planting movement in Corinth with this simple statement: "I planted the seed, Apollos watered it, but God made it grow" (1 Corinthians 3:6).

What does this mean to us? God is the creative energy behind these stories—He causes the growth. But that doesn't mean He does it all on His sovereign own. "All this is from God, who reconciled us to Himself through Christ and gave us the ministry of reconciliation" (Corinthians 5:18).

We ordinary humans have received the unfathomable ministry of reconciliation from the hand of God. These stories don't unfold without us. We may plant or water, but these stories demand us to play our parts. I have met many Muslims who've had a bona fide dream of Jesus but didn't really know what it meant. It sure made my job easier when I explained the Gospel to them, but if I didn't they may have gone to their graves with this fond feeling toward Jesus and nothing else.

With heaven's joy at stake, we can't afford to be stingy. For every one Desto there are many more Brams. The disappointing stories of rejection or attrition have the potential to deaden our hearts, but we must keep searching as the Good Shepherd does. Though they may be hard to find, there are fertile fields still out there. The motivation to keep searching for them, to keep scattering seeds, to keep slogging through all the disappointments, comes straight out of the heart of God.

You really do have the power to rock heaven with joy. You can bring a smile to the face of the Father by joining Him on seek and save missions into the lives of the desperate.

Send Us Out

A window in Scripture opens to reveal God's heart for desperately lost people:

> Jesus went through all the towns and villages, teaching in their synagogues, preaching the good news of the kingdom and healing every disease and sickness. When He saw the crowds, He had compassion on them, because they were harassed and helpless, like sheep without a shepherd. Then He said to His disciples, "The harvest is plentiful but the workers are few. Ask the Lord of the harvest, therefore, to send out workers into His harvest field." (Matthew 9:35-38)

Jesus sees and sighs. He even weeps. He takes to heart these harassed, helpless and shepherd-less sheep.

Then we feel the gaze of the Good Shepherd moving toward us. He's got a look of determination in His eyes. He's already been preaching the Good News of the kingdom and healing every disease and sickness. He's on a desperate search and His heart will not be deterred.

And now we hear His commanding voice. He's summoning us to join with Him and get our boots dirty, too. He sends us into the messy lives of the desperate. He trains us up into a life of prayer, calling for more reinforcements. "Send out more workers" becomes our frequent cry.

The work is hard. But the Lord of the harvest has promised to be with us even as He sends us out into His own harvest field. We know that the reward will be well worth it: the joy in our master's eyes over lives redeemed.

Lord, here am I. Thank You that You searched for me and sought me out. Compel me with Your love into a life of imploring others into Your kingdom. I confess I can't do this with my own will power or self-efforts. I need You. I want to be fueled by the joy of heaven today. Send me out with Your compassion and boldness to this world that You so love.

EPILOGUE

———

RESCUED

I looked with the captain out into the darkened horizon as salty mist sprayed into both of our faces. Again I muttered the same prayer that God would make a way where there was no way, just to make double sure He heard us.

About two minutes later the captain pointed to a light on the horizon and I asked what it was.

"A ship," he answered. "It looks like a big ship."

My heart soared. I asked him if this could be the U.S. Navy? He shrugged and said he didn't know, and then sent the vessel an S.O.S. message with his headlamps. We got closer and saw that it was an Indonesian Navy ship, a 1950's Russian-made clunker used mainly for cargo transport. We were permitted to dock alongside it. All of us, somewhat drunken from seasickness, climbed the rope ladder from our boat to the ship, which was full of refugees and boxes of supplies, and met a smiling crew who seemed excited to rescue a group of foreigners.

One of our delirious teammates thought he was climbing the rope ladder to the U.S.S. Lincoln, which was also sailing in the Indian Ocean for the relief work. He was imagining warm food and a warm bed and maybe even an internet connection to send word home. When his head cleared the side of the boat, it was met with a strong blast of diesel smell and the sight of hundreds of ragged refugees lying on dirty cardboard mats. Nope, this ain't the Lincoln.

We all began making a bed for ourselves on the oily deck among the boxes and displaced people. They were so kind to us, even offering to place folded cardboard boxes under our heads as pillows. The captain quickly came out to us and he offered the use of his VIP room. Amazingly, he was a believer in Jesus (in a predominately Muslim county) and very much wanted to show us hospitality.

Our team settled down for the night in the cramped room and most of us eventually stopped vomiting. We were so grateful to be out of the body bags and that the worst nuisance now was hearing loud snoring. The next day we got showers and the crew fed us a hot breakfast. We were all in jovial spirits, talking about our exciting adventure the night before which now seemed movie-like funny.

It was a moment of giddy joy for a rescue from God. He had made a way where there was no way.

The laughter evaporated quickly when a group of Indonesian ladies with sad faces entered the VIP room to have breakfast with us. One older lady related a story of how she was consumed with worry since the tsunami hit, thinking about her children who lived along the coast. Through tears she told us how she took a bus from Jakarta and had been traveling for four days on her search. Other girls were looking for their parents.

We could only offer listening ears and prayers for them to find their loved ones. It immediately made us somber again—this wasn't about our team having an exciting, fun-to-tell adventure but about showing the love of God to people who had suffered in ways beyond imagining.

After a few more travel adventures we finally got our team to the village and set up our medical clinic. The lines were long.

They still are. The harvest is plentiful. The laborers are few.

Can you cry out to God with your own desperation, and then reach with His love into the desperation of others?

ACKNOWLEDGMENTS

I started this book to help me process the desperation in my own life. I'm so grateful to God that He doesn't leave us alone in these desperate places, but reaches into our lives with rich community so we walk through to the other side together. Thanks so much to my loving family and faithful friends on both sides of the Pacific. I couldn't ask for a more excellent, Jesus-loving and Kingdom-advancing tribe.

A special, extra thanks for the superb feedback and editing help from Tim Stewart, Robyn van Leeuwen, Dave Thomas, Melissa Nelson, Debbie Wittig, Katie Hope, Sabrina Stolle, Crystal Kehn, Suzanne Van Hoorn, Kyle Miller, Jim Walter, Angie Payne, Meagan Brown and Patrick and Kim Duffy. I appreciate your help and treasure your friendship!

ABOUT THE AUTHOR

Mike O'Quin Jr. served as a social entrepreneur in Indonesia for 14 years with his family. He currently lives in Southeast Asia where he serves in a pastoral role for an international missions organization.

Mike is married to his high school sweetheart Stephanie and together they have four kids, three grown and out of the house and one teenaged one still tagging along. He can still make all of their eyes roll with his corny dad jokes.

You can follow Mike on Instagram @mikeoquin, Twitter @mikeoquin, and find him on his blog at mikeoquin.com

OTHER BOOKS BY MIKE O'QUIN JR.

Unearthing Heaven: Why Tomorrow's Rewards Matter Today

How would your life on earth be different if you thought about your reward in heaven more?

Christ taught often on heaven's rewards, and the early church reveled in this treasure chest of life motivation. Throughout church history, Jesus' followers have been captivated by a coming event known as "The Judgment Seat of Christ," a place of reward and honor at life's finish line which inspired them deeply. We moderns, not so much.

Why is that? Why do we brush away heaven's rewards, seeing them as possibly selfish or even unspiritual? Or maybe we don't think about them at all, surrendering them to stale stereotypes about heaven.

Unearthing Heaven takes you on a journey to rediscover this lost treasure chest of life motivation. Mike unpacks the two metaphors the Apostle Paul used to help us understand this Great Day, and looks into the four crowns of the New Testament, each one championing a different Kingdom value. You'll see how mediating on this glorious future event can even loosen the grip of common life struggles. Stir your imagination for the Day when you stand before Jesus and see a smile on His beaming face, hearing Him declare, "Well done, good and faithful servant. Enter into the joy of your master" (Matthew 25:23).

MIKE O'QUIN JR.

Java Wake

Stephen Cranton's mid-life crisis is coming on a decade too early. On a business trip to Indonesia, he evaluates his heartless existence after getting challenged by an obnoxious adventure guide on his flight. Soon after landing, Stephen tries to spice up his stale life with a brazen act of spontaneity. Bad move. His impulsiveness sets off a chain of events, one that brings enemies into his life and endangers new friends. His longsuffering wife, who makes a spontaneous move of her own by flying to Java for a last-ditch marriage intervention, also gets tangled up in his miscalculation. Stephen feels like he is living inside a nightmare that he can't seem to escape, but will the ordeal be enough to wake up his sleeping heart?

"An atmospheric debut." – *Kirkus Reviews*

ENDNOTES

1 Commonly attributed to Henry David Thoreau, in a later paraphrase that sprang from his quote on desperation in an earlier edition of *Walden* (Boston: Ticknor and Fields, 1854).

2 John and Staci Eldredge, *Captivating: Unveiling the Mystery of a Woman's Soul* (Nashville: Nelson Books, 2005).

3 C.S. Lewis, *God in the Dock,* (Grand Rapids, MI: Eerdmans, 1970)

4 Dr. Seuss, *How the Grinch Stole Christmas,* (New York: Random House Books, 1957)

5 *You're a Mean One, Mr. Grinch,* Composed by Albert Hague, Performed by Thurl Ravanscroft for the 1996 cartoon special, *How the Grinch Stole Christmas.*

6 *Dr. Seuss' How The Grinch Stole Christmas,* Directed by Ron Howard (Universal Studios, 2000).

7 Paul Richardson, from an earlier manuscript of *A Certain Risk* (Grand Rapids, MI: Zondervan, 2010).

8 Philip Yancey, *What Good Is God?: In Search of a Faith That Matters* (Nashville: FaithWords, 2013).

9 Mary Forsythe with Beth Clark, *A Glimpse of Grace* (Dallas: Kingdom Living Press, 2002).

10 Ibid

11 Ibid

12 Jonathan Edwards, editor. By David Brainerd, *The Life and Diary of David Brainerd,* (Charleston, SC: CreateSpace, 2012)

13 Ibid

14 I highly recommend Jim Walter and his amazing team at the Center for Relational Care in Austin. See more at www.relationalcare.org

15 Gary Thomas, *Sacred Marriage: What If God Designed Marriage to Make Us Holy More Than to Make Us Happy?* (Grand Rapids, MI: Zondervan, 2008).

16 Anonymous, from personal email to Mike O'Quin

17 C. S. Lewis, *Mere Christianity* (New York: MacMillan Publishing Company, 1952).

18 Gary Smalley, *Secrets of Lasting Love: Uncovering The Keys To Lifelong Intimacy* (New York: Simon & Schuste, 2001).

19 *Joe Versus The Volcano*, Directed by John Patrick Shanley (Warner Brothers, 1990).

20 Floyd McClung, *Living on the Devil's Doorstep*, (Nashville: W Publishing Group, 1988).

21 *Chasing the Dragon*, Jackie Pullinger (Ventura, California, Regal Books, 2004).

22 Presentation Elevation, a graphic design outsourcing company that was located in Indonesia.

23 Bryan L. Myers, *Walking with the Poor: Principles and Practices of Transformational Development* (Maryknoll, NY: Orbis Books, 1999).

24 David Ferguson, *The Great Commandment Principle* (Carol Stream, IL: Tyndale House Publishers, 1998).

25 Ibid

[26] Kyle Miller, director of Global Care & Response. See more of their amazing ministry to hurting people on their Facebook page or at www.globalcareresponse.org

[27] Ron Parrish, *From Duty to Delight: Finding Greater Joy in Daily Prayer* (Lititz, PA: House to House Publishers, 2006).

[28] Email from a friend serving there, who needs to remain anonymous for security reasons

Made in the USA
Las Vegas, NV
11 May 2022

48775831R00101